JUN 2005

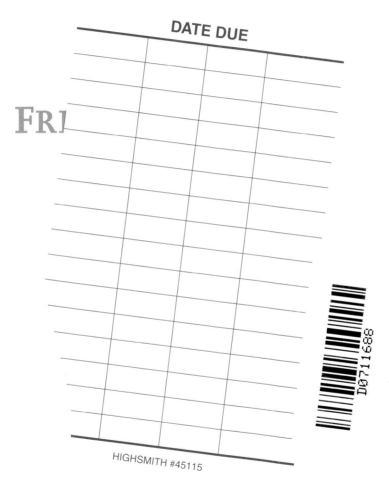

DATE DUE

FRI

HIGHSMITH #45115

D0711688

FRIENDS ARE
Everything

BJ Gallagher

CONARI PRESS

First published in 2005 by Conari Press,
an imprint of Red Wheel/Weiser, LLC
York Beach, ME
With offices at:
368 Congress Street
Boston, MA 02210
www.redwheelweiser.com

Library of Congress Cataloging-in-Publication Data Available Upon Request

Typeset in Joanne, Mural Script, and Veljovic by Suzanne Albertson

Printed in Canada
TCP

12 11 10 09 08 07 06 05

8 7 6 5 4 3 2 1

The paper used in this publication meets the minimum requirements of the
American National Standard for Information Sciences—Permanence of Paper for
Printed Library Materials Z39.48-1992 (R1997).

For Anita Goldstein, Susan Goldstein, Jeanne Segal,
and all the other fabulous, brilliant, talented, creative,
generous, loving women in the Brain Exchange.
My life is richer because of you!

Contents

Introduction

The universe is made up of stories, not of atoms.
—MURIEL RUKEYSER, poet

This is a simple, heartfelt book about one of the most important aspects of my life—friendships. Here I have collected stories and poems from my friends, from their friends, and I have added a few stories of my own—all in an attempt to distill wisdom about what it means to be a true friend. Others' stories are signed with their names; my own stories are unsigned.

Friends are everything . . . and everywhere. We are related to our friends by heart—and sometimes by blood as well. Friends can be neighbors, coworkers, classmates from grade-school days to college daze, bosses, sisters, mothers, sons, brothers, fathers, kith and kin. Friends share our good times and our bad, joining us in laughter as well as tears.

The subject is both broad and deep, and one small book cannot possibly hold all there is to know about friendship. But perhaps, if I have done my job well, I have captured some pearls of wisdom, a few golden nuggets of insight, a handful of friendship gems to treasure.

This book of stories is my gift to my friends, past, present, and future. As Pearl S. Buck famously said, "Strangers are simply friends I haven't met yet." What do you mean to me, dear friends? Let me see if I can begin to tell you . . .

Trust

Respect

Understanding

Empathy

Forgiveness

Responsiveness

Insight

Expressions of love

Needing one another

Dependability

Spiritual connection

True Friends

Understand that the little things can make a BIG difference

Sometimes when we are generous in small, barely detectable ways, it can change someone else's life forever.

—MARGARET CHO, comedian

How Do You Love Me?
Let Me Count the Ways.

WHEN I THINK ABOUT all the ways in which my friends show their love for me, it is many of the little things that come to mind:

- Ruby and Paddy, who live next door and feed and watch over my five cats whenever I go out of town . . . so I can travel with peace of mind, knowing that my beloved, furry, four-footed family is safe and secure at home.
- My friend Diana, who often leaves a flower or a sprig of berries on my gate at night, just to let me know she's in the neighborhood walking her dogs . . . and thinking of me.
- My artist friend Antonette, who made some fabulous papier-mâché eggs one Easter and left them in a basket on my doorstep before dawn . . . just to wish me a happy Easter in a very special way.
- My writing partner Steve, who, when I send him an e-mail joke, always has to have the last word—so he tops the joke with a punch line that is better than the original . . . leaving me laughing out loud in the solitude of my office.
- My mother Gloria, who occasionally slips a $20 bill into her letters to me—"mad money," she calls it. Mom has always been one of my best friends.
- My friend Joan, whose quips and quotes, those pearls of wisdom, have guided and inspired me over the past twenty

years. . . . I could write a whole book on the many things I have learned from Joan!

- My friend Anita, who welcomes me into her Berkeley home whenever I am in northern California and need a place to stay . . . and if she's out of town, she just leaves me a key so I can stay there anyway!
- Two of my son's former girlfriends, Nancy and Yvonne, who still send me cards on Mother's Day (even though Michael long ago married someone else). . . . I still think of those two girls as the daughters I never had.

What do these friends all have in common? They understand that it's the little things, the simple things, the thoughtful surprises that express love and friendship best. These little things make a BIG difference in my life!

Plant a seed of friendship; reap a bouquet of happiness.
—Lois L. Kaufman, author, humorist

True happiness is of a retired nature, and an enemy to pomp and noise; it arises, in the first place, from the enjoyment of one's self, and in the next from the friendship and conversation of a few select companions.
—Joseph Addison, English essayist, poet, politician

Sister

Where are you now, *babita*, companion,

amiga, my friend?

Didn't we sit the winter through,

snowflakes melting on our tongues,

waiting for summers' lilies to hold our dreams?

How we loved

the bullfrogs and the toads. Ah, dear one,

I hope you remember

I touched your shoulder with my heart.

—Janell Moon

HELPING HAND: *What's in a Word?*

Hearing what's needed

Eager to contribute

Listening with compassion

Paying attention to the little things

Intuitively understanding what's helpful and
   what's not

Never overstepping your bounds

Going out of your way for a true friend

Healing love, healing touch

Asking "What can I do to help?"

Never assuming that you know what's best

Desiring to serve and contribute to others' well-
   being

*You have not lived a perfect day . . . unless you have
done something for someone who will never be able to
repay you.*
   —Ruth Smeltzer, author

Statistics of Hope

Every seven minutes, somewhere in the world, someone is falling in love.

Every six minutes, two women pour tea and sit down for a good talk.

Every five minutes, someone, somewhere is doing a good deed.

Every four minutes, someone stops and says, "Thanks, I needed that."

Every three minutes, someone hugs someone else in need.

Every two minutes, someone comforts a crying child.

Every minute of the day and night, somewhere in the world, someone is at prayer, saying,

"Thank you . . ." to the Sacred Mystery which sustains us all.

—Christina Baldwin, from *We'Moon '98*

Boomerang Zucchini:
The Gift That Keeps on Giving!

MANY YEARS AGO I LIVED in Minnesota on a lot big enough to have an old-fashioned garden. Minnesota has a pretty short growing season, so it's difficult to grow some things. But not zucchini, which proliferates, and will even "volunteer" the next year if you leave the squash in the garden.

So this year we began giving away zucchini as fast as we could—to all our coworkers and neighbors and friends. And pretty soon it started coming back—sometimes as dinner invitations at which zucchini made an appearance: the big ones hollowed out and stuffed with a delicious meat mixture, the little ones cut into sticks and served raw as crudités. Or delivered to our front steps—all different kinds of zucchini bread, with and without nuts, and even zucchini chocolate cake. Yum!

It seems like such a little thing—zucchini making the rounds in our neighborhood. But as I look back, those were some of the best memories I have of that summer and that community. I still smile whenever I see zucchini today!

—Jane Bjorkman

Book Party

ANYONE WHO'S EVER TRIED to get a book published knows how much rejection is involved in the process. When I wrote my first book back in the mid-'80s, I got dozens of rejection letters, one right after another. I often got discouraged, would give up, and stop sending out the proposal. After a few months, I'd get another burst of enthusiasm and send it out again. More rejection . . . more depression and resignation . . . then another round of optimism and sending out the proposal.

The book was finally accepted by a tiny little publishing house in St. Louis, and in 1985, my first book came out. To celebrate the occasion, my friend Gary threw a book party for me. He rented a room, arranged the catering, and invited all my family and friends—it made me feel so good. The best part was that he took the dozens of rejection letters I had received and enlarged them on a copy machine. He made big posters out of them and used them to cover the walls of the room in which the party was held. It was hysterical. A small thoughtful, creative gesture—but it was perfect. He reminded me that in the midst of much rejection, it's essential to persevere—all I need to find is just one "Yes."

Think big, start small.
> —Patricia Fripp, author, speaker

Girl Scout Forever

THE CHILDHOOD FRIENDSHIPS I made in the Girl Scouts have lasted for more than twenty years. Twenty years of big events in each others' lives—as well as little things that brought us gales of laughter and colorful memories. I recall when one of the girls got married . . . at the reception the rest of us donned our Walawi jackets over our formal wear and pulled out our green Walawi songbooks, mess kits, and badge-covered mugs. As we sang "We Really Do Need Each Other," one of the girls' husbands snapped away with a disposable camera that had been placed on the table. Then we stole the groom away, made him replace his tuxedo jacket with a Walawi jacket, and made him pose like he was in a re-dedication. It was hysterical—a wedding reception no one will forget. It's the little things like that—the zany, crazy, fun things that girls do—that make our lives so much richer.

—Tori Kay Radaich

Remember, the greatest gift is not found in a store or under a tree, but in the hearts of true friends.
—Cindy Lew, author

Bad Hair Months

TWENTY-EIGHT YEARS AGO, I was pregnant with my daughter. It was a difficult pregnancy. I was quite sick in the early part. Then, late in the pregnancy, my hips started to dislocate and I had low blood pressure, so I was apt to faint. Worst of all, to my mind, was that my hair looked so horrible. Brittle and dry—I'd never had hair like that before. One morning, in my eighth month, I went out to go to work and there was an envelope tucked under my windshield. In it was a beautiful red cotton scarf with delicate green and yellow flowers. A friend left it in the night, with a note attached about how she hoped the bright colors would cheer me up. I tied it around my hair and wore it for most of the next month. I still have that scarf. I plan to give it to my daughter one day.

—Jane Bjorkman

Fearless

I WENT TO THE MAILBOX, and there inside was a fat little envelope addressed to "The Amazing, Talented BJ Gallagher." "What could this be?" I wondered to myself, smiling in anticipation. Must be something special, for sure. And indeed it was.

Inside was a card, a very funny refrigerator magnet, and a sparkly beaded bracelet that said F-E-A-R-L-E-S-S. What a great gift! It was from Diane Conway, who wrote a wonderful book called *What Would You Do If You Had No Fear?* I had written an endorsement for her book, and the bracelet was a token of her thanks. I promptly put in on my wrist and haven't taken it off since. The FEARLESS message resonated with me—reminding me how much courage it takes to face life, to embrace its challenges, ride its ups and downs, lick our wounds, fall down, pick ourselves up, take risks, make leaps, and keep going no matter what. While I wear the bracelet on my wrist, its message I carry in my heart.

I called Diane to thank her for the delightful gift, and I asked her to tell me about the bracelets. "I started making them three or four years ago," she said. "I made them to give to special friends who needed encouragement. I also make some that say M-I-R-A-C-L-E, and I give those to people who need a miracle in their lives."

"I'm sure it makes a huge impression on people when you give them one of your bracelets," I said.

"Yes, it does," she replied. "Some people cry, lots of them hug me, and people often write me letters about what the bracelet means to them, and how it gave them just what they needed in a particular moment."

"It's such a little thing," I said. "A single, stretchy thread of beads with a word spelled out—but it's loaded with such significance and meaning for people."

"Yes, you're right," she replied. "Some people need a miracle and others need to be reminded to be fearless. These days, I give them to complete strangers . . . especially to people I see who seem to be hanging on by their fingernails and who clearly need a miracle."

"Where do you get the bracelets?" I asked Diane. "Do you buy them or make them?"

"I make them all myself—I make about five every evening, while I'm watching TV or just relaxing with my husband," she answered. "Each one is a little different and each one is handmade with love."

"The power of little things," I mused.

"I'm hoping these little things will lead to something big," Diane said. "I'm going to start making kits, and make them available so that other people can make FEARLESS and MIRACLE bracelets and give them to still more people. I'd love to start a revolution—a Fearless Revolution. Wouldn't that be great?"

"Yes, it would," I said softly. "It would be very great. I'm thrilled to be a part of that revolution. Thank you for my bracelet. I will wear it fearlessly and spread the word."

Where there is a woman there is magic.
—Ntozake Shange, poet, playwright

If one is lucky, a solitary fantasy can totally transform one million realities.
—Maya Angelou, poet, author

True Friends

Laugh together . . . often!

Laughter is the closest distance between two people.
—VICTOR BORGE, Danish-born comic pianist

More Fun Than a Barrel of Monkeys

KATIE AND I WERE THE TWO assistant store managers for the local I. Magnin department store. We had become good friends over the course of working together, and we had lots of wonderful fun.

Katie's responsibilities included the children's department. One season we had an oversupply of small stuffed toy monkeys called "Monkey Do's." She had sent her boss, Jay, the store's general manager, a memo alerting him to the problem, including a tongue-in-cheek warning that "if you don't take care of this problem, it will multiply."

A couple weeks went by, and Jay did not respond. Katie got an idea. Late one night after closing, she and I gathered up about fifty of these monkeys and snuck into our boss's office. We festooned his entire office with these stuffed critters. We put one on his phone, another on his computer, several on his book cases, in his files, and we even put some of them in obscene positions—fornicating monkeys in the middle of his desk! And we left a note that read, "If you don't take care of your problems, they multiply."

Now this boss of ours—while he did have a sense of humor—was very serious about his job. He was German, very proper and dignified, and he played his role of corporate executive to the hilt. As I think back on it, Katie and I were living dangerously in pulling a prank on such as him. But we lived to tell the tale.

You should have seen his face the next morning at 7:15 when he arrived at his office! And much to our surprise, he didn't call us on the carpet. In fact, he was so amazed (and, I think, secretly delighted at our spunk) that he called his boss, Gerald Napier, the president of I. Magnin, to come to his office and have a look. The two of them—and the two of us—got a great laugh out of the escapade.

Just thinking about it makes me laugh all over again. Ahhhh, memories!

—Kitty Cole

You will do foolish things, but do them with enthusiasm.
—Colette, French novelist

One doesn't have a sense of humor. It has you.
—Larry Gelbart, comedy writer

Why Did the Chicken Cross the Road? . . .
To Get Away from the Door!

ONE OF THE THINGS I love the best about my friend, Arleen Gevanthor, is the way she makes me laugh. She regales me with stories that are like something out of a movie—and, better yet, they often have a little nugget of wisdom buried in them.

One of my favorites is about the pet chicken she had as a girl. The chicken was an indoor/outdoor bird, having the run of both the house and the yard. One Sunday, Arleen's large extended family had gathered together to enjoy the afternoon and to share dinner. Arleen's mother, aunt, sister, and the family maid were all in the kitchen, preparing the evening meal. At one point, her aunt went out the kitchen door to get some herbs from the garden and accidentally let the screen door slam behind her. Unbeknownst to her, the chicken, who was right behind her, got hit in the head by the closing door. When her aunt came back toward the house, she saw the chicken's limp body at the bottom of the steps. She picked it up and tossed it into the trash. A short while later, Arleen's mother came to the back door to take some trash out. Seeing the chicken's body in the trash, she picked up the lifeless fowl and carried it back into the kitchen and put it on the counter. She was not going to waste a perfectly good chicken, even if it had been a family pet. When the maid saw the limp chicken on the counter, she figured it was just knocked out. She gave it half an aspirin. Ten minutes later, the chicken regained consciousness and was on its feet again, running around the kitchen.

Arleen's chicken story speaks volumes about these three women—Arleen's aunt, her mother, and the maid. Each saw the same problem but had her own interpretation of the situation and what to do about it. Arleen's aunt, who didn't look beyond the obvious, took one look at the chicken, and deciding it must be dead, trashed it. Arleen's mother, a thrifty woman who wasted nothing, decided to make a meal of the lifeless chicken. And the maid, being an optimist, decided to be resourceful and try to save the chicken with aspirin.

Arleen's chicken story is a parable about how people act on their perceptions of life events. Some simply take things at face value—they just accept things as they perceive them. Others might ask themselves, "How can I make the most of this situation?" and look for a creative response. And still others don't accept the obvious, but rather try to change a bad situation (revive the chicken)—they know "it ain't over till it's over."

What I love best about the story is the way it made me laugh—I could see the whole scene unfolding in my head. Thanks for the laughter, dear friend. I needed that!

Laugh at yourself first, before anyone else can.
　　—Elsa Maxwell, gossip columnist, songwriter,
　　　professional hostess

Among those whom I like or admire, I can find no common denominator, but among those whom I love, I can: all of them make me laugh.
　　—W. H. Auden, writer

Laughter is inner jogging.
　　—Norman Cousins, editor, writer

Whoever is happy will make others happy too.
　　—Anne Frank, German diarist

I finally figured out the only reason to be alive is to enjoy it.
　　—Rita Mae Brown, author, social activist

Long-Distance Laughter

MY FRIEND MARGARET AND I haven't lived in the same state since 1986. But we've managed to stay close—going on trips together, seeing each other at least once a year at her house or mine. She loves coming to visit me as a respite from her large extended family—husband, four children, their spouses, nine grandchildren, and dogs and cats (oh my)—who live near her. I live alone in a city I haven't lived in for very long. She likes the peace and quiet, while I relish the visits to her house where every night seems like a dinner party.

Recently Margaret has taken up the habit of noticing something she's never seen before in her sixty-some years on this planet. Some little thing. I've tried to convince her she should write these down—some of them are priceless. But her idea of what to do with them is to tell them to me—or to leave them as messages on my voicemail. Recently I came home to a message that went something like this:

"Well, I saw something today I'd never seen before. I saw a young man standing in front of a window. He looked around to see if anyone was there, then spit into his hands, a big gob of viscous stuff and then smoothed his hair back. I'm pretty sure he didn't see me seeing him because he did this twice."

By the end of the message I was laughing so hard I had to put the phone down. And, if it doesn't seem funny to everyone, well, that's because senses of humor—like friendships—are all different.

—Jan Johnson

Humor is just truth, only faster!
—Gilda Radner, comedian, actress

LAUGHTER: *What's in a Word?*

Loving life, with its ups and downs

Appreciating what's right with the world

Understanding your own quirks and eccentricities

Going for the gusto (and the guffaw!)

Having fun wherever and whenever you can

Taking life seriously, but taking yourself lightly

Eager to embrace life's lunacies

Ready to grin at every opportunity

If you don't learn to laugh at trouble, you won't have anything to laugh at when you're old.
> —Edgar Watson Howe, journalist, author

We cannot really love anybody with whom we never laugh.
> —Agnes Repplier, essayist, humorist

Be happy. It's one way of being wise.
> —Colette, French novelist

Finding "Mr. *Probably* Right"

THE QUEST FOR LOVE, romance, dates, sex, and/or marriage has been a regular subject of my women's group (the Brain Exchange) over the years. Some women are looking for husbands; some are struggling with the husbands they already have; and some are recovering from husbands they just divorced. Some of us could care less about husbands—we're interested in lovers, partners, romantic interludes, or some other type of affair of the heart.

In my own search for "Mr. Right," my friends have been an important source of emotional support, as well as practical, down-to-earth advice. I've asked them to brainstorm about where and how to meet wonderful men; how to evaluate the ones I attract; how to deal with my own anxiety and ambivalence about intimacy; and how to break off a long-term love affair that clearly did not have the future potential I desired. Some of their ideas were serious, others ridiculous, and still others sublime.

One of the most creative ideas was to make a colorful book cover with a bold title, *Looking for Love in All the Right Places,* wrap the book cover around whatever book I happen to be reading, and carry it with me wherever I go—airports, restaurants, conferences. Boy, it has been a great conversation starter! . . . but not a relationship starter.

Another friend suggested I join a synagogue and let the rabbi know that I wanted to get married. Someone else in the group went one step further and told me to join an *orthodox* synagogue—that way, the rabbi and the women of the temple would make *sure* I got married . . . and *stayed* married! All the women in the room laughed. When I reminded them that I wasn't Jewish, one retorted, "Never mind, that's a different issue!" Gales of laughter ensued.

I made a commitment to Internet dating because of the encouragement—no, nagging—of women in the Brain Exchange. Several of them had met the loves of their lives on the Internet, and one woman even wrote a book telling how to do it—it was called *Putting Your Heart On Line*. I finally decided that all those friends must be right, and I signed up for a couple of Internet dating services. (I never did join a synagogue, but I did the next best thing—I signed up for jdate.com, an Internet dating service for Jewish singles.)

Thanks to the encouragement of my friends, I have met many great guys doing this Internet dating thing. I've had lots of laughs . . . but some tears too. Still, I'm not giving up on the online dating, since my friends reassure me that it's a numbers game. "Go out on enough dates," they say, "and one of them is bound to be Mr. Right. It's the Law of Probability."

"OK. So I'm looking for Mr. Probably Right?" I reply. It would be funnier if it weren't so true.

I'm not offended by all the dumb blonde jokes because I know I'm not dumb . . . and I also know that I'm not blonde.

—Dolly Parton, singer/songwriter, actress

If evolution was worth its salt, by now it should've evolved something better than survival of the fittest. . . . I think a better idea would be survival of the wittiest.

—Jane Wagner, playwright

Daffy about Ducks

IT ALL STARTED WITH this life-sized white plastic duck (or is it a goose?) dressed in hunting gear—camouflage jacket, hunter's hat with flaps over the ears, and a pop-gun rifle. It was hysterical. I found it in a local gift shop, and I thought it was just the funniest thing. So I bought him, and put him out on my front porch.

The saleswoman in the shop had lots of other ducks as well, dressed in various seasonal costumes. These were duck-dolls for grownups—you buy one duck, then buy different outfits so you can change his (her?) clothes with each season. A Santa outfit for Christmas, a pumpkin costume for Halloween, the hunter's get-up for fall, a businessman's suit and hat for all-season wear, and a pink furry bunny costume for Easter. Ever seen a duck dressed like a rabbit? Oh my. I'm clearly a women with nothing better to do with her time and money than play dress-up with a plastic duck! In case there is any doubt about my eccentricity . . . after a couple months, I bought a *second* one, so I'd have one for each side of the porch.

I've had these ducks for five or six years, faithfully changing their clothes with each season. And when I got bored, I'd go out and buy a new duck outfit to cheer myself up. There were summer frocks with big straw hats, a witch's costume, a couple of darling Valentine's outfits, and the cutest blue fuzzy bathrobe, complete with curlers under a scarf to tie on the duck's head and a tiny hairdryer tucked in the pocket of the robe.

It was always easy giving people directions to my house. . . . "Just look for the porch with the ducks in drag," I would tell people. My neighbors joked about the ducks, and I withstood merciless teasing, but I didn't care. I was having fun, so I just let their teasing roll off my back.

My cousin gave me a third plastic duck—this one had a hole in his back so he could be filled with soil and a plant. She was so pleased with herself for finding this unusual duck. Just what I needed—a mutant duck with a geranium growing out his back.

A couple years ago, I got tired of changing the ducks' clothes all the time, so I packed their wardrobe away in a box, and just left them naked on the porch. Then I had the yard fenced and decided to reposition the ducks, peering out between the slats in the fence. They made a friendly greeting team, I thought. Now my neighbors teased me about having all my ducks in a row!

One morning, I noticed something was awry with the ducks. One of the ducks was no longer peering out the fence, but turned away instead. "Hmmm, who moved my duck?" I wondered. I turned him around and put him back in place. The next morning, one of the other ducks was out of position. "What the heck . . .?" I wondered. This happened for the next several days. Each morning, one of the ducks would be moved . . . showing up in different parts of the yard. And in the following week, two or sometimes all three of the ducks had been moved! What was going on here?

I wondered who it was orchestrating my ducks around the yard. After falsely accusing my cousin, my next door neighbors, and my son, I finally zeroed in on the real culprit—my friend John Lawton who lives down the street. His dog and my dog are best friends, and he walks his dog early every morning, long before we are awake. That's when he did his nefarious duck wrangling. He seemed to have them engaged in some kind of silent tableau, acting out a story. The duck with the geranium in his back was ostracized by the other two, and they turned their backs on him. Then one duck would go hide from his friends. Then one would hide in the bamboo and be peeking out to see if they could see him. It was all very funny.

"Well, two can play at this game," I thought. So I started moving the ducks around, too. It became like a game of duck-chess, each of us trying to outdo the other with some imaginative placing of the ducks in my yard. When John and I would happen to see each other walking our dogs in the evenings sometimes, we'd laugh about the ducks and wonder aloud, "What would happen next?"

Then one week, I went out of town on a business trip. I was gone four days, and when I came back, there were only two ducks in my yard, one of whom was standing on my porch with a laminated sign hung around his neck with string. The sign was a ransom note, cut and pasted words from magazines, which read, "If you ever want to see your precious duck again, wait for the call." I laughed my head off. "This couldn't have been pulled off by just one person," I thought. "Clearly, John must have an accomplice helping him now. His wife must have joined in the trickery." There was nothing for me to do but wait for the call.

The call came one evening a couple days later. "Do you miss your precious duckie?" a nasal voice hissed over the phone.

I played along. "Who are you?" I yelled with mock seriousness. "Who are you and what have you done with my duckie? Have you killed him? Put him on the phone. Let me talk to him."

The voice hissed back, "There is a ransom to be paid. If you want to see your precious duckie again, bring a bottle of chilled champagne Friday night, at 5 P.M., to the fourth driveway down the street."

"How do I know he's still alive?" I faked crying now. "How do I know you haven't turned him into Peking duck?" I pretend-sobbed.

"Just be there Friday," the voice hissed, and he hung up.

"This guy has clearly gone 'round the bend," I said to myself as I hung up the phone. But I was still laughing.

Friday night came and I showed up at 5 P.M. in John's driveway with my dog and a bottle of chilled champagne. He opened the door and invited me in, using that weird hissing voice from the phone calls. He invited me out to the deck, where his wife Terri sat with my kidnapped duck. On the patio table was a wonderful spread of cheeses, crackers, olives, crudités, and bottles of wine. John announced that this had been his last day of work and he was now officially retired.

"What a way to arrange for a retirement party!" I told him. The three of us enjoyed a lovely evening of wine, nibble food, and conversation, while our dogs played in the yard and we laughed about the great duck adventure.

The latest chapter in our duck drama came just a few months ago, on the morning of my birthday. At 5:30 A.M. my dog started making a ruckus like she heard something outdoors and wanted to go take care of it. I stumbled out of bed and to the door, turned off the alarm, and let the dog go out. I closed the door and headed back to bed. At 7 A.M. I got up, went out to get the paper, and discovered that the duck wranglers had been at it again. A big banner was affixed to my fence with a string of pink balloons. The banner read, "Happy Birthday from the Dukz." There were colorful little party hats on each of the ducks, who were gathered around a bottle of champagne. I just shook my head and laughed. What a way to begin my birthday! It was bound to be a good one, with this auspicious start.

I've had lots of wonderful friends and neighbors over the years, but none who have ever made me laugh so much, so often. What on earth will those ducks do next?! Thank you, John and Terri, for the love and laughter you bring to my life. You may be a little daffy, but I couldn't ask for better friends!

Wit has truth in it; wisecracking is simply calisthenics with words.
—Dorothy Parker, satirical poet, writer, critic

He who laughs, lasts.
—Mary Pettibone Poole, writer

True Friends

Help us see ourselves more clearly

I can trust my friends.
These people force me to examine,
encourage me to grow.

—CHER, singer, actress

My Friend, the Mirror

MY FRIEND LORRIE MCGRATH gives me one of the most important things that a child needs from her parents, but often doesn't get—mirroring and positive reinforcement. She helps me see things in myself that I can't see by myself. She reminds me of what I do well.

It happens most often in work situations. When I'm having a problem with one of the people who work for me, I often tell Lorrie how I'm dealing with it. She'll say, "You're always so good at that. It's just like that time when you handled that other problem . . . you know, the one with Susan a couple of years ago."

"Gee, I hadn't thought about it," I reply. "But now that you point it out, I guess you're right."

"I've always admired the way you handle that kind of problem," Lorrie continues. She mirrors my good side back to me in a way that is so uplifting and affirming. It's the kind of thing I should have gotten from my parents, but didn't. Many of us don't.

Sometimes when I am stuck and don't know what to do, Lorrie says, "That sounds like the same kind of problem you had not too long ago with X, remember? Maybe you could resolve this problem in a similar way. What do you think?" She reminds me of my past successes, then encourages me to use the same skills to be successful in the present situation. It's mirroring in a coaching kind of way.

You know how parents admire a piece of art work that their daughter brings home from school, no matter what it really looks like? "Oh, sweetheart, that green doggie is so beautiful, and that purple sun with the pink clouds is so artistic—I just love it!" is what every child needs to hear. It's what I needed to hear when, as a teen, I painted the dashboard of my car blue and put pink polka dots on it. But that wasn't the reaction I got from my folks, for sure!

What makes Lorrie such a true friend is that she loves me unconditionally. In fact, I'm sure if I called her up and said, "Guess what? I just robbed a bank," she would probably reply, "Well, it probably needed to be robbed. I'm sure they had too much money in there."

Lorrie does other amazing things as my friend, in addition to the mirroring—things that continuously remind me how much she loves me. I told her how much I loved my hot tub, and so she went out and bought one for herself. Now, almost every time I talk to her, she says, "I was sitting in my hot tub the other night and thinking of you. I'm so grateful you told me about hot tubs!"

Lorrie is very spiritual, and she tells me that she's praying for me. Lately, my life has been just fine, so I tell her to "save the prayers for when I really need them!" And we both laugh. A true friend like Lorrie is just a gem—a rare treasure, a magic mirror, like something out of a fairy tale. Mirror, mirror on the wall, who's the luckiest friend of all? I am!

—*Dana Kyle*

I want to be all that I am capable of becoming. . . .
—Katherine Mansfield, New Zealand-born writer

Don't compromise yourself. You're all you've got.
—Janis Joplin, singer/songwriter

The Dance of True Friends

ANITA GOLDSTEIN AND SUSAN GOLDSTEIN are not biological sisters, but they are certainly sisters in spirit. They were the first women who came to mind when I was thinking of writing a book about friends. They epitomize everything I want in a friend—especially a kind of easy, seamless way of being with one another. Anita often jokes, "Susan is the other half of my memory. She can finish my sentences; she can give me the word I'm looking for and can't quite reach; she remembers points that I'm trying to make in a conversation and makes them more beautifully than I would."

Anita tells me, "One of the things that makes our friendship so easy—it's one of great lessons I've learned from Susan—it has to do with respecting boundaries."

Susan joins in, "We never get mad at each other. We often do things together, but if Anita asks me to do something and I don't want to do it, I simply say so. I don't feel like I have an obligation to do everything together—if an activity works for me, then I go, and if it doesn't, I don't. I don't have to be overly polite or make excuses."

"And that's impressive, because Susan is really polite," Anita replies. "She is always tactful with people—she's not as blunt and outspoken as I can be." They both laugh.

Anita and Susan met in 1981 at the Santa Monica home of mutual friends, Jeanne and Robert Segal, at a planning meeting for the Association of Humanistic Psychology (AHP). Susan was in southern California visiting her friend, Victor Herbert, and he took her to one of the planning meetings on a Monday night. Susan was new to the group, so when they arrived, Victor introduced Susan to Anita by saying, "Anita, this is Susan. Take care of her." Susan jokes, "And Anita's been taking care of me ever since!" They laugh again.

Susan continues, "Anita and I complement each other well. She knows how to do things that I don't know how to do." Anita corrects her: "I do things that Susan *thinks* she doesn't know how to do!" Still more laughter.

ANITA: "Look, we each have areas where we're not totally self-confident . . . despite the fact that we may *look* self confident."

SUSAN: "Anita is especially fun to go clothes shopping with. When I was a girl and would go shopping with a family member, their response was always to point out what was wrong with something . . . 'Oh, the sleeves are too long on this; it'll have to be altered,' or 'You don't have anything to go with that color,' or 'This part doesn't fit quite right; that'll never do.' It was always negative, and the shopping was never fun. Anita on the other hand, will do just the opposite. . . . 'That color looks great on you; I'll bet you have something at home it will go with,' or 'This part is a little loose, but that's easy to fix,' or 'Let's find something to wear with this, so you'll have a complete outfit.' It's always positive. All I have to do is stay in the dressing room and Anita will scour the racks to find just the right thing, and bring it to me. It's great."

ANITA: "Not atypical for families, I would imagine. They always point out what's wrong with us, or what we're doing that they think is a mistake. That's why we need friends—because friends always point out what's *right* with us and what we're doing!"

"When I listen to you two," I tell them, "it makes me want to pack up and move to Berkeley to be close to you. You have got to be two of my all-time favorite women!"

Susan replies, "Well, that's exactly how Anita came to live here! Every time she would come up from Los Angeles for a visit, she would say, 'This is really wonderful. I could live here. I just love being around you.' Then when her son and daughter-in-law, who live in Sonoma, had their first baby, Anita and Paul packed up and moved here. Now we're less than a mile from each other."

"Well, if we keep talking like this much longer, I'll be moving up there too! Just one question—should I change my last name to Goldstein, too? So there'll be three of us Goldstein girls?" Gales of laughter follow.

God gives us our relatives. Thank God we can choose our friends.

—Ethel Watts Mumford, novelist, humor writer

Lenses Unlimited

Friends are like a magnifying glass. . . . They show us things we don't notice ourselves.

Friends are like having eyes in the back of your head. . . . they point out what you can't see . . . help you with your blind spots.

Friends are like periscopes. . . . They can help you see around life's corners. Maybe they've been there/done that . . . like thinking they could change the boss. Maybe they've got some objectivity and emotional distance . . . like seeing that boyfriend for what he really is.

Friends are like good reading glasses. . . . They help us decipher the fine print.

Friends are like bright, shiny mirrors . . . reflecting back to us how beautiful we really are.

—Jane Bjorkman

Please, Help Me Stop
Shooting Myself in the Foot!

I WAS IN THE UNFORTUNATE POSITION of working for two executives who were both weak and ineffective. They were nice enough guys—but they weren't very talented or bright. I had developed the dangerous habit of complaining about my bosses behind their backs. It made me feel better to complain to my friends, and I secretly hoped that word would get back to the president of the company and that he would do something about my terrible bosses.

My complaining backfired. Not only did the president not fire my bosses, he took me aside and told me to stop bad-mouthing them. I learned the hard way that loyalty is one of the key values of the good-ole-boy system. Even if someone is incompetent, it is unseemly to diss them openly.

I shared my problem with my friend Bonnie. I had jeopardized my career chances within the organization. I was getting the cold shoulder from some of the other execs. "I don't get it," I complained to Bonnie. "I do a great job with my work, but I happen to report to a couple of numbskulls, and when I point out that 'the emperor wears no clothes'—I am the one who gets punished, not the incompetents!"

Bonnie explained the situation this way: "Executives like to work with people who make them feel good about themselves. In fact, *everyone* likes to work with people who make them feel good about themselves. Your complaining about your bosses has made many of the executives uncomfortable around you. Your bosses have heard your complaints through the grapevine, and they don't like it. And their boss (the president) feels uncomfortable because he knows he should do something, but he isn't prepared to at this point in time. Your complaining puts him on the spot. And the other execs are nervous because you might start bad-mouthing them too. In short, the guys don't want you around because you don't make them feel good about themselves. It's a very human thing—it's not just executive men who are like this."

I was sobered by this assessment. I knew my friend was right, but I didn't know what to do about it. The damage was already done. If only someone had taught me things like this *before* I went into the business world.

I realize now that business is a game. The players learn the rules and play by them. The problem is, most of the rules aren't written down anywhere, so we have to figure them out on our own, or by watching others. And all too often, we don't know there *is* a rule about something until we find out the hard way by breaking it!

It was a painful lesson, but my friend Bonnie gave me the feedback I needed to stop shooting myself in the foot and to learn from my mistakes. I realized that my mother was right when she tried to teach me, "If you can't say something nice, don't say anything." I wish I had listened to Mom. But I didn't, so at least I'm grateful I had a friend like Bonnie to teach me as an adult what I had refused to learn as a child.

—Maxine Lum

The smart teacher knows her job.

The clever teacher knows her employer.

The intelligent teacher knows her subject.

The brilliant teacher knows her students.

The wise teacher knows herself.

—Carolyn Gage, from *We'Moon '98*

Feedback Is the Breakfast of Champions

A FEW YEARS AGO I had a conversation with a girlfriend—it didn't go well. I went to great lengths to be tactful with my friend, because I knew she was sensitive and got her feelings hurt easily. I can't even remember now what the conversation was about, but I do remember that the outcome was less than wonderful.

Later that same day I had a conversation with my son Michael. He is an unusually wise and insightful young man, and I count him as one of my closest and most trusted friends. I decided to ask him for his perspective on my unhappy experience. I told him the subject of the conversation, and I explained how carefully I had chosen my words as I talked with my friend. I told him the whole story, including the awkward ending as my friend and I got off the phone. Then I asked, "What went wrong?"

Michael thought for just a moment, then asked me a question: "Mom, who were you being in that conversation?"

"What do you mean, 'Who was I being'?" I replied.

"Who were you being? Were you being 'Listen to me because I'm smarter than you'? Were you being 'Let me tell you how to solve that problem'? Were you being condescending, or arrogant, or righteous?" he queried.

"Does it sound like I was?" I asked.

"What do *you* think?" he answered.

I had to think about that for a minute or two. "Well, yes, I suppose I was," I reluctantly admitted.

"That's what went wrong," he said. "The problem isn't in *what you were saying*. The problem is in *who you were being* in that conversation."

"Oh," I acknowledged. "No wonder the conversation didn't go well."

"Uh-huh," was his only comment.

Michael's words continue to come back to me on many, many occasions. "It's not what you're saying, it's who you're being." So simple, so profound . . . so helpful.

Aren't I lucky? One of the unexpected bonuses of parenthood is having my child grow up and turn into a best friend!

The most exhausting thing in life is being insincere.
    —Anne Morrow Lindbergh, writer, aviator

Out of the Mouths of Babes

I WAS TELLING MY GROWN SON (now my friend) about an annoying heckler who was giving me a hard time while I was doing an author event at a local Barnes and Noble. I was conscious of asking the heckler to leave with an open heart—an idea from the book I was presenting.

As I was relating the incident to my son, it occurred to me that I had already told him about it before . . . so I asked if I had.

He said, "Well, Mom, if you need to tell me a story three or four times, I figure it's really important."

Patience. He didn't learn that from me.

—Janell Moon

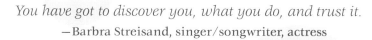

You have got to discover you, what you do, and trust it.
—Barbra Streisand, singer/songwriter, actress

My Friends Keep My Doubts
and Demons in Check

AS IF WE DIDN'T HAVE ENOUGH of a challenge dealing with the external obstacles and problems that life throws our way—we've got internal obstacles, too! Sometimes the biggest problems we have to deal with are in our own heads. Or as Pogo famously said, "We have seen the enemy, and it is us!"

My friend Connie said recently, "I have a *dybbuk* in my head. I went to the doctor the other day for some medical tests. I only have to pay 20 percent, since my insurance picks up the rest. But when the receptionist handed me the bill for my share of the tests, I about fell over! It was so expensive! The receptionist told me that the next round of tests were going to be even more expensive—and I decided right there and then that I would *not* have any more tests. Those prices are just ridiculous! But then later that same afternoon I found myself in the parking lot of a local coffee shop, rifling through the car trunk of a woman who sells knock-off designer handbags. I was grabbing them up as if my life depended on getting enough of them!" She looked at me and shook her head. "I can't believe the way my mind works. There is definitely a *dybbuk* in my head, a demon that makes me think in crazy terms!"

And it's not just about money that we have crazy thoughts—we have all sorts of creative rationalizations for all kinds of things:

- Claudia thinks out loud, "Pizza is good for you because it has all the basic food groups—grain (wheat crust), vegetables (tomato paste), protein (pepperoni), dairy (cheese), and just a little touch of oil. Heck, it's downright health food!"

- Cherize tells herself, "Well, I ate something I shouldn't have eaten at lunch, so now I've blown my diet. . . . I might as well give in and eat whatever I want for the rest of the day. I'll start my diet again tomorrow."
- Izumi storms, "I had a terrible argument with my ex-husband, so I'm going to go buy our son an expensive present, just to show who really loves him!"
- Elena decides, "I don't have time to clean the whole house today, so I won't clean any of it. I'll wait until I have time to do the whole thing really thoroughly."
- Pat muses, "There's this little chunk of cake sticking out on the edge like that—I might as well cut it off to even it out— just a little slice won't hurt. I just want the edge to be even and smooth."
- Marsha tells herself (and her husband), "Look how much money I saved! The shoes I wanted were on sale, half-price, so I bought three pairs in different colors. I saved so much money!"

These and other women have taught me that the voices in our heads are often not wise, sensible voices—in fact, they are quite the opposite! Sometimes the voices in our heads are seductive sirens— they sound good, but they lure us into self-destructive behavior.

The "Worry Wart" is one of these voices: "What if something bad happens? What if I get fired? What if my boyfriend finds somebody else? What if I don't have enough money when I'm an old lady? What if my best friend gets mad at me?"

The "Alarmist" is a sister of the Worry Wart: "Be careful! The world is a dangerous place! Don't do this . . . don't do that! Don't go there, it's too dangerous. Don't wear your nice jewelry to the grocery store—somebody might knock you over the head and take it. Don't go out at night! Don't go to that part of town! What, are you crazy? Don't even think about doing that!"

"Never Enough" is the voice of insecurity and scarcity: "Better buy it now—it won't be there later. Hold on to the boyfriend you've got—he may not be the greatest, but he's better than no boyfriend at all. I'd better not give this money to charity—I might need it myself. Never pass up free food; always clean your plate. Better save this (fill in the blank)—ya never know when you might need it."

And "Self-Doubt" is arguably the worst voice of all: "Be on your good behavior. If people find out what you're *really* like, no one will like you. Don't say what you really think—you might annoy someone. I could never do X—I'm not smart/talented/capable enough. I'm not good enough to get the job/boyfriend/opportunity that I really want. I might as well not even try."

What I've learned from listening to the voices in my own head and listening to my friends talk about the voices in their heads is that we all have a cacophony of voices going on in our heads all the time. It's like a Greek chorus, providing background music to conversations and action on the main stage.

The *good* voices in my head—the clear voice of Intuition and the strong voice of Reason—are the voices I want to listen to. When I heed them, I am steered in positive directions and I make good choices for myself.

How do I sort them out? How can I avoid listening to the whisperings and lamentations of my Greek chorus, and turn instead to the good voices in my head—the voices of *Love, Hope, Possibility,* and *Promise?*

Over the years, my friends have taught me that the best thing I can do is to have a conversation with someone about whatever is on my mind—career goals, financial decisions, health concerns, worries about relationships and family. Engaging in a real dialogue with a trusted friend is my best insurance against the Greek chorus gaining control of my mind. A good companion is essential for a safe journey through reflection to the destination of decision. I've learned from my friends that "the mind is a dangerous place—don't go in there alone."

Never mistake knowledge for wisdom. One helps you make a living; the other helps you make a life.
—Sandra Carey, author

In a friend you find a second self.
—Isabelle Norton, author

4

True Friends

Love us unconditionally,
just as we are

Oh, the comfort, the inexpressible comfort of feeling
safe with a person, having neither to weigh thoughts nor
measure words, but pouring them all right out, just as
they are, chaff and grain together; certain that a
faithful hand will take and sift them, keep what is
worth keeping, and then with the breath of
kindness blow the rest away.
—DINAH MARIA MULOCK CRAIK, poet

Friends, Not Judges

DON AND MARILYN WERE THE BEST neighbors I ever had. They did the stuff that all good neighbors do—they helped out when my babysitter cancelled at the last minute, they brought food when I was sick, they picked up my mail when I went out of town, they watered my plants, and neighborly things like that. But they did something else too, something special and quite extraordinary. They accepted me just as I was, and befriended me in a way that I have rarely experienced.

I was going through a very difficult time in my life: I was twenty-three years old, recently separated from my husband, who lived on the opposite coast; I was raising a four-year-old son and going to college full time; and I was going through what's commonly known as post-divorce craziness. I was drinking too much, dabbling in soft drugs, inviting men home, throwing wild parties. I had missed the '60s and the sexual revolution, and I was bound and determined to make up for lost time. (This was in the early '70s, when sex was safe and cars were dangerous, unlike today, when the opposite is true.)

Don and Marilyn were evangelical Christians, just about as squeaky clean as you can get. They were a traditional family with a stay-at-home mom who kept a perfect home and cooked great meals every night, three beautiful wholesome kids, and a father who brought home the bacon. They were like something right out of an old TV show like *Father Knows Best*, or *The Donna Reed Show*. They went to church every Sunday and said grace before meals.

I, on the other hand, was a single mom going to college, dressed in jeans, Army shirts, and Earth Shoes™. I fancied myself something of an "Earth Mother," baking my own whole wheat bread, fermenting homemade wine in the back bedroom, and shopping at the local food co-op for honey, cheese, dates, and fresh peanut butter.

Every day I rode my son to day care on the back of my bicycle, then I pedaled off to my day of classes at the university. After class, I hung around the local student pub and had a few beers with graduate students and some of my professors.

The only thing I had in common with my neighbors, it seemed, was parenthood and geographical proximity—they lived upstairs in my apartment building.

And yet this wonderful couple invited me (and my young son) for Sunday dinners and holiday meals. My own family was far away, so Don and Marilyn opened their home and their hearts to me as if they were my family. My lifestyle was clearly at odds with theirs, and yet they never once criticized or scolded me. They never preached at me, either. Instead, they *lived* their Christian faith, exemplifying one of Jesus' teachings: "Judge not, lest ye be judged." Don and Marilyn loved me unconditionally, just as I was.

We lost touch over the years, and I don't know where they are any more. I moved across country, to bring my son closer to his dad and extended family and to finish my education at another university. But wherever they are, I hope they know how much I loved them, and how much I appreciated their unconditional acceptance.

I learned an important lesson from them, a lesson that I try to live in my own life: honoring and respecting others for who they are, while refraining from judging and criticizing. I am committed to being a friend, not a judge.

UNCONDITIONAL: *What's in a Word?*

Unlimited love

No judgment or criticism

Constancy over time

Open arms, open mind

No strings, limits, or prerequisites

Doing what's right

Intent to listen and learn

Time and attention generously given

Interdependence

Open heart, open home

Needing one another

Affirming others' goodness

Loyalty in good times and bad

A woman who is loved always has success.
—Vicki Baum, Austrian-born writer

A Best Friend's Legacy

THE YEAR MY BEST FRIEND DIED, I asked why of everything; I wanted the world to be thrown to my feet in answers. Those early days I couldn't manage a journey so delicately webbed. I didn't yet know that sometimes troubles are beyond solution. I prayed for grace to walk with me so I could bring it home to her through prayer. And I knew her spirit, no matter how burdened, always had love for me.

One day, after feeling unsafe in the world, thinking it was possible for the bay to hurl its water up the legs of my house, bury my velvet chair and fill my broom closets, I realized the life I knew to be my story was gone. Homeless, I walked to the shore and sat on the rocks to hear the prayer from my body, but the rock was cold and unwelcoming and the water silent. I felt alone with grief.

I turned to a support group for people who had lost loved ones in difficult circumstances. I heard tales of nests full of stones, lost mates and children, the eggs of their hearts broken. It was pain that made me belong; we all wanted resurrection from pain. I took my deep yearning for healing to people who understood my heartache and set me free, for it was in their human nature that I found the kernel of forgiveness for Suzanne for harming herself, and for myself and all that I didn't do to help.

I let myself imagine I could touch the light in the trees and ride it. I realized Suzanne's spirit could be in the trees. With prayer, I understood I didn't have to understand; I could simply pray for happiness of life and a release of suffering. I prayed for my loved one to be in a gentle woods and felt her spirit near. I let the time come when she seemed settled among the blowing grasses and even the tree near my office. I let her be part of my spirit prayer life.

Looking back over our twenty-seven-year friendship, I realized we had given each other a steady branch from which to live out our dreams. I encouraged her to quit her secure administrative job at a community college and become a hypnotherapist. She did, and she was so much less stressed working with people one on one and making a contribution in a personal way. She found creative ways to work with people in classes and said she felt truly connected for the first time. She encouraged me to join a performance art group with her; how she loved the stage, while I was entranced with the writing. What a surprise for me! It soon became apparent that I had a special "poetry ear," and Suzanne was my biggest fan when I started submitting my work.

A year after the breakup of my marriage, I called her one night and told her I had met a woman I was attracted to. Although it was close to midnight, she said to hurry home and we'd have a good talk. She was so loving and supportive of any choice I made, and I'll always thank her for that.

Today I look back on our times together and think of her as the sister I never had, the mother I always wanted, the friend I had only read about, and the godmother who looked out for my good. In return, I gave her the poetry of North Beach, the art of the absurd, the wing of a hawk, and my shoulder to lean on.

I live in a condo her inheritance helped me buy, with a large black Madonna ceramic piece in my garden. The black Madonna is the guardian of the harbors, and every time I look at it, I feel gratitude for our relationship that made us both risk more, hurt more, and, in the end, live better.

—Janell Moon

The depth of a friendship—how much it means to us . . . depends, at least in part, upon how many parts of ourselves a friend sees, shares, and validates.
  —Lillian Rubin, psychotherapist, author

I always felt that the great high privilege, relief, and comfort of friendship was that one had to explain nothing.
  —Katherine Mansfield, New Zealand-born writer

All of It

The night after Suzanne died
my dreams blaze of light,
shutters opening and shutting,
then tunnels of fog
leading to mirrors and crystals.
Something in my body
knows she is not mine.

How can I erase the memory
of this last year?
Why should the ending
be the measure of her life?
I didn't save her
from the fast-rushing days.
My body says over
and over, she is not mine.

Her mind exploded into angel-sickness.
I didn't know how to give her the earth.

My prayers say her breath belonged to her,
that each of us has the right not to suffer.

Her life, she'd want you to remember,
was filled with years of song and taffy.

—Janell Moon

Silences make the real conversations between friends. Not the saying but the never needing to say is what counts.
—Margaret Lee Runbeck, author

Time to Take Off the Mask

I CRIED ALL THE WAY HOME from the party. The man that I was deeply in love with had been there . . . with a date. I was devastated. Jack and I had broken up some months earlier, and I was still grieving the end of our love affair. I knew that he would be at the party, since this was a celebration for faculty and graduate students in my department at the university, and he was a faculty member. So of course he would be there. But I thought he would come alone. How could he show up with a date?

But I never let him, or anyone else, see my pain—in fact, just the opposite. I was at my charming best. I looked great, wearing a new outfit I had bought for the occasion. I was funny, entertaining, the life of the party. I regaled everyone with great stories and jokes, flirting at every chance, and putting on quite a show. I made sure that people had a great time.

Then the evening was over and I drove home, alone. Sobbing all the way, I felt hurt that no one comforted me in my pain. Why didn't they see through my act? I asked myself. Why didn't someone take me aside and reassure me that it was going to be OK, that I was going to be OK?

The next day I had lunch with my friend Don Miller. My eyes were still red from the night of crying. I complained to him about how unhappy I was that none of my friends at the party had supported me in the way I wanted them to.

"Why would they?" he asked me. "You were giving them all a great time. Why would they want you to stop?"

I was stumped. "I don't know," I replied.

"Here's the deal," he explained. "You make life wonderful for your friends by always being 'on.' You put on your beautiful mask, you're charming and funny, and you've trained them to see you in this way. It's not *their* fault that you're putting on an act. It's your fault. You've done this to yourself. You can't blame them."

Well, Don had me there. He was right. I had created this delightful public persona that now I felt compelled to maintain, under all circumstances. What could I do?

"Why don't you try just being yourself?" he suggested in that soft, gentle way of his. "Try it a little bit at a time. See what happens."

What did I have to lose? Nothing but the burden of being constantly charming. So I tried it. The next time I was depressed, I just showed up the way I was. I watched to see if any of my friends turned away. Nope. They were still my friends. And they accepted me whether I showed up happy or sad. What an amazing discovery! Gradually, over time, I was willing to reveal more and more of what I was feeling. And still no one ran away from me. It took several years of slowly revealing more and more of who I really was, and what was going on with me, to come completely out of my emotional closet.

My friend Don gave me a lovely gift—the gift of being myself.

Real charity and a real ability never to condemn—the one real virtue—is so often the result of a waking experience that gives a glimpse of what lies beneath things.

—Ivy Compton-Burnett, English novelist

Detach with Love

I used to think that I was supposed to help protect my loved ones from going down wrong paths and making painful mistakes. But I've discovered that interfering with others' life experiences is not really helping them—often it's doing them a great disservice. Pain is the touchstone of personal and spiritual growth—our suffering is actually a gift, teaching us important lessons. As Mark Twain wisely said, "A man who carries a cat by the tail learns something he can learn in no other way."

I suspect that my attempts to rescue or save others are really motivated by the desire to avoid my own pain, because seeing the pain of someone I care about is upsetting to me. But as I become more willing to experience my own sadness, fear, upset, and grief, I understand that pain is a normal part of life. When I accept that fact, I am more trusting that others can handle their own pain.

It is loving and respectful to allow my loved ones to live their own lives and experience the consequences of their actions. I can love and support others, but I mustn't try to control or fix them. The best thing I can do is to keep my hands off but keep my heart turned on. It may be painful for both of us, but in the long run, we'll both benefit.

One is taught by experience to put a premium on those few
people who can appreciate you for what you are. . . .
—Gail Godwin, writer

I'm treating you as a friend, asking you to share my
present minuses, in the hope that I can ask you to
share my future pluses.
—Katherine Mansfield, New Zealand-born writer

Allowing Our Friends the Dignity of Their Own Choices

THIS HAS BEEN A TOUGH LESSON FOR ME to learn—one that has taken years. It was my dear friend Karen Cutts who said to me simply and quietly one day, "We must allow our friends the dignity of their own choices."

How many times in the past have I tried to talk a friend out of something I was absolutely sure was the wrong thing for her? How many times have I told a girlfriend that she could "do better" in her choice of a boyfriend or husband? How often have I tried (with nothing but the best of intentions, of course) to tell a friend how to run her career, her finances, her marriage, her family, her health . . . or all of the above!? I shudder to think of all the advice I've dished out to dear and wonderful friends who didn't need or want my advice.

But it's never too late to learn, thank goodness! Karen prompted me to ask myself several questions:

- Do I like it when friends and family try to tell me what to do?
- Do I appreciate unsolicited advice and opinions from others?
- Do I ever take their advice?
- Do I resent others for trying to tell me how to live my life?

My answers were No, No, Rarely, and Yes.

So what makes me think that others are any different from me? Shouldn't I get out of the advice business and get into the love business instead? Absolutely! I need to close my mouth and just open my heart.

Thanks to the lesson Karen taught me, the past few years have been characterized by remarkable peace and freedom. It's remarkable how much time and energy I have now that I'm not trying to tell people how they should live their lives! They are free to make their own choices, and I am free to make mine. Together, we enjoy friendships of acceptance, dignity, freedom, and love.

I have learned that to have a good friend is the purest of all God's gifts, for it is a love that has no exchange of payment.

—Frances Farmer, actress

True Friends

Teach and inspire us to be our best selves

*Always be a first-rate version of yourself,
instead of a second-rate version of somebody else.*
—JUDY GARLAND, singer, actress

Tag! You're It!

I'VE HAD SEVERAL STAGES in my career: In my early twenties I was in public relations at Rockefeller Center. Then I spent nine years as a Navy nurse. Finally, I worked at a fine civilian hospital in San Diego for twenty years, until I retired. In each of those three stages, I was blessed to have a significant friend teach me something profound— something that would affect and shape the rest of my life.

At Rockefeller Center I worked for Caroline, the director of public relations. She was a powerful woman—ahead of her times in many ways—and a warm, loving mentor to me. I had grown up in a strict family, so Carolyn's unquestioning love and support was a welcome change from the environment I was used to. It wasn't so much what she *said*, it was more a matter of what she *did*.

For instance, just days before I was to be shipped overseas for my first tour as a Navy nurse, I stopped by her office, in uniform, to say good-bye. With an appraising glance at my attire, she gave me my marching orders. "Go to the Music Hall and take in the show. Then meet me for dinner in the Rainbow Room." I did as she suggested. That evening, when I walked into the Rainbow Room, the orchestra leader looked up, nodded at me, and then led the orchestra in the score from *South Pacific*. I was so touched. Caroline knew how to express her loving support in so many creative ways. She became a lifelong friend. I love her dearly and am forever in her debt for lessons learned about surprising another with love.

Later, as a young ensign, I reported to a lieutenant commander named Vi. One day she walked across the compound to the nurses' quarters. When she saw me, she said, "Lorrie, I was looking for you. I heard what a wonderful job you are doing with that Cardiac Unit. I wanted to tell you about it." I was amazed. She could have waited until the next time she saw me—or she could have made a mental note to tell me later. Instead she went out of her way to walk across the compound to give me a word of praise. This impressed me so much and made me feel so special. Vi and I stayed in touch for many years, and I consider her my friend, though she was also my boss.

Vi was a strong role model for me—a model of the power of positive reinforcement. I often remark to others, "You know, people stand in line for 45 minutes to register a complaint about something, but they won't take 5 minutes to give someone a compliment!" I still look to catch my friends and others in the act of doing something marvelous that I can call their attention to or sing their praises to their bosses. People need that kind of attention so much, especially those whose job it is to help you. So, I tell my friends, "Don't stop with giving them a tip. Tell their boss what a great employee they have!"

The third friend who helped me enormously is Helen, director of the Heart Patient Project at Sharp Hospital, where I worked the last part of my career. I was working on my master's degree and trying to decide on the subject for my thesis. She suggested a great topic (aphasia), and I followed up with it. When I got an A on my thesis, I went to see Helen to say "Thank you."

"No," she replied.

"No?" I asked, confused.

"No," she said again. "It's tag. You're 'it.'" She made it clear that, rather than give my gratitude to Helen, it was my job to pass along the good deed.

In the military, you don't have the luxury of spending years and years with people, developing friendships. But our friendships are long lasting in a different way. We may not see each other for a long time, but when we do, it's as if the other woman had gone down to the corner to buy a newspaper. We just pick up right where we left off.

That's how I feel, especially about these three important friends. Each one of them left an imprint on my life—a legacy that I've been able to pass along to other friends along the way. Our friendships are ongoing, deeply seated, profoundly felt. Each friend gave me a gift that it is my duty and my delight to continue giving to others.

—Lorrie McGrath

How we treasure and admire the people who acknowledge us!

—Julie Morgenstern, author, speaker, professional organizer

Attitude Adjustment

PAUL STROUP AND I WERE GREAT FRIENDS—we met and hit it off instantly. What struck me when I first saw him was that he and I looked so much alike, he could easily have been my brother. Tall, blonde, blue-eyed, smart, funny, and articulate—I thought perhaps we were twins separated at birth. He seemed to be a male version of me.

Paul and I worked together for several years, traveling around the country conducting seminars for one of the Big Three auto manufacturers in Detroit, teaching their car salesmen to be nice to customers. We enjoyed training together and became as smooth as Ginger Rogers and Fred Astaire—dancing our way through our two-day seminars, week after week, month after month.

Paul was the consummate professional—doing the same impeccable work consistently, day in and day out. I, on the other hand, was getting bored. I could conduct those seminars in my sleep—I was restless and distracted. I spent more and more time out in the hallway, talking on the phone, trying to assuage my boredom with interesting conversations.

One afternoon, Paul gave the group a break. As usual, I was in the hallway on the phone. Paul sauntered up to me, sipping a Coke as he waited for me to finish my call. When I got off the phone, he draped his arm around my shoulder in a brotherly way and said, "BJ, you need an attitude adjustment." I didn't have to ask what he meant—I knew.

His comment was a verbal kick in the butt—just what I needed to snap me out of my malaise. He told me the truth about myself—I was slacking off, lowering my standards, not doing my best job for the client, and letting Paul down as well. I felt guilty and embarrassed. I mumbled a lame apology to Paul and went to get a soft drink myself. But I got the message, loud and clear. And I responded. As we completed the seminar that day, I was back in top form—attentive, involved, committed to doing a great job for our client and our students.

Paul's words sometimes come back to me—when I'm in a funk, working on a boring project, or dragging my feet about something I really don't want to do. "BJ, you need an attitude adjustment," I will tell myself, seeing Paul in my mind. And then I grab my head with my hands over my ears, and give my head a quarter turn, complete with creaking sound effects, to physically turn my attitude in a different direction. Paul would laugh if he ever saw me do it.

I don't think I ever told him how much his honesty meant to me that day, and how much it means to me still. He moved to Hawaii a few years ago, so I never see him any more. But he's in my mind still, chiding me gently. Thanks, Paul, I needed that.

Only friends will tell you the truths you need to hear to make . . . your life bearable.
—**Francine du Plessix Gray, Polish-born writer**

The Friendship

There is only dance
through changing of place;
so one day you
are the healer,
and the next,
the wounded child,
and by turns it
is my time to be
lost and find
home in your eyes,
or to give you a
flower of peace.
Solemnly we join
the pace, learning
the steps in silence,
each
wondering if the
other hears and feels
how tender,
how like a strong
river
is the tune.

—Jean Clayton, from *We'Moon '98*

My Friend/My Teacher

MY FRIEND BARBARA AND I fought many battles together in our twenty-five years of teaching. As first-year teachers without any job security, we protested at school against the war in Vietnam. We campaigned in many ways for services for women students on campus and fought to create a women's studies program at our college.

Although we often car-pooled, and belonged to various groups together, we were primarily professional friends. We talked about teaching a lot and we team-taught many times. She taught me, by her example, most of my important lessons about being a teacher. Early on in our careers, she asked me to observe and give her feedback about a class she thought wasn't going well. This impressed me enormously. Here was a woman who took charge of her own professional development and solicited the feedback she needed and wanted to become a better teacher. Although I have observed many teachers during my career, hers was the only request that was not instituted by some administrative requirement.

She was a courageous leader on campus and served as president of the Faculty Senate and later as chair of the Social Sciences Division. In these roles she spoke up on all kinds of issues, for which she often took a lot of heat. I admired the way she always acted with courage and integrity.

When she was dying of cancer, at much too young an age, I struggled over how to say good-bye and how to say something about what she meant to me. In our last conversation, I tried to avoid saying good-bye by saying, "You have been the person at school closest to me in terms of values. I'm so grateful for having you as a colleague."

Even in this last conversation, she taught me something important. She replied, "Oh, I always feel like what was valuable to me was when you and I *disagreed*. I always learned so much from that."

—Susan Goldstein

I believe that we are always attracted to what we need most, an instinct leading us toward the persons who are to open new vistas in our lives and fill them with new knowledge.

—Helene Iswolski, author, social activist

Yin and Yang

RANDY AND I COULDN'T BE more different. You'd think working with someone so different would make me crazy. And I must admit, in the beginning, it did. I am outgoing, talkative, high energy, and proactive, while Randy is introverted, somewhat aloof, and reactive. He likes to call me a Hokey Pokey person—and he's definitely not.

When I first hired him, I was doing all the marketing for my consulting business, as well as all the consulting itself, and I was feeling spread way too thin. I hired Randy so that I could turn the marketing over to him. Being the extrovert that I am, marketing was one of my strengths, and I found it hard to let go. I second-guessed everything that he wanted to do. We clashed often. But one of Randy's strengths is patience, and he hung in there with me. Over time, trust developed, and I was able to let go, let him do what I had hired him to do.

Our relationship got smoother. The differences that at first had caused irritation were now a source of balance and enrichment. We started writing together. I would do the research and lay out the elements—Randy would add flesh to the bones. I would start a sentence—Randy knew how to finish it. I would write a paragraph—he would add two sentences that made my original point even stronger. I like to say that "Randy writes Leslie as well as Leslie."

Over the years, our work relationship grew and evolved, and a friendship blossomed. We now understand each other as well as, and sometimes better than, we know ourselves. We serve as mirrors for one another. When Randy was having difficulty with angry parents challenging his soccer coaching of their children, I was able to be a mirror to help him see how he might have contributed to the situation—as well as to think through ways he might solve his problem. When I was having trouble with a client, Randy was able to be a mirror for me, to see my part in the conflict—and to explore possibilities for resolving it.

Randy and I are different in many ways, but one way in which we are not different is the way we both value fun—in our work and in our personal lives. Life is too short not to have fun, and we both try to live this in everything we do.

When we consider a new work project, we ask, "Would it be fun?" When we think about doing something together as friends, we ask, "Would it be fun?" If the answer is No, we usually don't do it. If the answer is Yes, then it's a no-brainer—of course we do it!

Our differences, which started out as a challenge, have turned into the glue that holds us together. We complement one another. Where I zig, he zags. Where I am yin, he is yang. Our friendship is definitely greater than the sum of its parts.

—Leslie Yerkes

We challenge one another to be funnier and smarter. . . .
It's the way friends make love to one another.
　　—Annie Gottlieb, author

dear wise one, crone teacher, and beloved friend,

i have seen you gliding in the cold river, more agile than many women much younger than you. your friends chuckle as they tell of your long bike trips—"don't dare offer her a ride in your car if it's raining!" they say, amused and amazed at your vivacious strength.

your smiles carry heaven to earth, and you show me what i wish to become. when i hear you laugh and say, "oh, there's plenty of time," i remember i don't need to rush. when i catch your glances of compassion as you honor those less able-bodied or less fearless than you, i learn reverence and love for all. as the fire in your speech and eyes reveals your passion, your concern for justice, your fierce independence, i am also enkindled. what greater wisdom than patience riding a flame of will?

from you i have learned silence, courage and the ways of nature—the wisdom of bending with the winds and floods i cannot change, the way to blaze like a golden poplar when all is dreary, and how to let go when ripeness arrives—and mostly i am learning, through reverence for you, to revere, at last, all that is.

for these great gifts, and more—always more—i thank you and bless you.

—helen laurence

The Bravest Woman I Know

LITTLE DID I KNOW THE EVENING that Brenda Knight and I met at Knoc Knoc (a trendy sake bar in San Francisco) that one day I would be sitting in a hospital with her, going through one of the most powerful experiences of our lives.

I had seen Brenda in so many different lights over the years. We worked together; we partied together; we were both single and dating. She had been there for me at an important turning point in my life—introducing me to her friends in San Francisco and making me feel welcome after I had uprooted myself from New York, leaving behind family and friends. We had grown close, sharing the ups and downs of life in the publishing biz, falling in and out of love, being there for one another, as good friends do. But nothing in our friendship prepared me for the powerful lesson in love I was to learn from Brenda during her bout with breast cancer.

When she was first diagnosed, I told her that I would do anything I could to support her and help her through this. I loved her like a sister—of course, I would be there for her. She asked if I would go with her when she had her mastectomy. "Which of my friends are responsible?" Brenda asked me rhetorically. "You're the only one." We both laughed, because we knew that wasn't true (though she did have a few flaky friends).

We went to the hospital that day, and sat in the waiting room along with another friend, chatting, laughing, reading magazines, gossiping, as if we were waiting to get our hair done. We all felt the tension, but we kept it light on the surface. I thought this was Brenda's breezy way of keeping fear at bay, and I was happy to play along.

A woman came into the waiting room to talk to us—she was from a breast cancer support group. She could support Brenda in ways that I never could, because she'd been through the experience herself. "I've had a double mastectomy—would you like to see the results?" We said Yes. The four of us were alone in the room, so she unbuttoned her blouse and showed us her breasts—her gorgeous, reconstructed breasts. That's when the reality of it all really hit me. I got a lump in my throat. Here we were, looking at what was ahead for Brenda—many surgeries and much pain later. What really struck me was the nipples—it had never occurred to me that when they remove your breasts and build you two new ones, they have to make nipples, too. There is no dark skin, so they have to use tattoos to make the new nipples more realistic. The enormity of what Brenda was facing was quickly becoming real to both of us.

The time came for her sedation before they took her away for the surgery. They injected an IV, and Brenda began to relax. I hugged her one last time before she walked down the hall to the operating room. For the first time, tears welled up in her eyes, and I realized that all morning she had been holding it together for my benefit. I began to cry, too. We held each other for as long as we could, then I watched her walk down that hall toward a surgery that would take most of the day. I cried as I realized that she was going in there all alone. No one could be there with her as she went under the knife. I felt so helpless.

I sat there in the waiting room all day with our other friend. We answered Brenda's cell phone dozens of times, as her many pals called on her "yak line." Her mom called. She lived far away and couldn't come to be with her daughter during the surgery. Friends called from all over—any one of whom would gladly have been there in the waiting room that day. There was such an outpouring of love and concern—it was very powerful.

As I look back and recall Brenda walking down the hall toward her surgery, I think, "There goes the bravest woman I know." All the time I thought I was taking care of her, I realize that she was taking care of me.

When the doctor came out to tell us that the surgery had gone OK, I was in my typical Jewish mother mode: "You have to be sure and tell her to take it easy—not to go back to work right away. You just make sure you tell her what to do—she'll listen to you—you're a doctor." I was beside myself with worry, adamant in telling him what to tell her.

The doctor just looked at me and said quietly, "Leslie, everyone gets through this in their own way."

I am so much in awe of Brenda. Others may not see what I see in her—it's easy to be fooled by her light, carefree manner. But she's substantial—she's a rock. She inspires me to be a better person. She is the bravest woman I know.

—Leslie Rossman

Friendship with oneself is all-important, because without it one cannot be friends with anyone else in the world.
—Eleanor Roosevelt, American First Lady,
humanitarian

There is often in people to whom "the worst" has happened an almost transcendent freedom, for they have faced "the worst" and survived it.
—Carol Pearson, author

You're alive. Do something. The directive in life is so uncomplicated. It can be expressed in single words. Look, Listen, Choose, Act.
—Barbara Hall, author

6

True Friends

Extend themselves with generosity and love

When you give each other everything,
it becomes an even trade. Each wins all.

—LOIS MCMASTER BUJOLD,
science fiction writer

A Temporary Solution Turned Into a Chapter in My Life

IT WAS THE YEAR FROM HELL—September 1993 to September 1994—the dog died, my marriage of twenty-four years ended, and my house burned down. I had moved into a new rented house with my youngest son, Sutton, after my husband and I split up. We'd been in the house just six weeks. I went to a dinner party one night, and as I drove home, I saw helicopters hovering in the general vicinity of my new home. Smoke was billowing into the sky, and sirens were wailing. As I got closer, I thought, "Wouldn't it be awful if that was my house?" Then I turned the corner, and sure enough, it was my house.

I was devastated. It had been such a horrible year, and now everything I owned had gone up in smoke. Mementos, baby pictures, family keepsakes, clothes, furniture—everything was destroyed. My marriage was gone, my dog was gone, my home was gone, and all my worldly possessions, except my car and the clothes on my back, were gone too.

My son and I stayed with a friend for a couple of nights. Then my friend Gail heard about the fire, called me up, and said, "Come move into my house. I have seven bedrooms and five bathrooms—plenty of space for you and Sutton." It was a sprawling ranch house on a double lot in La Jolla, with an ocean view, to boot. Gail had three kids at home, but there was still plenty of room for Sutton and me. Her offer was a godsend. Little did I know that her offer of a temporary place to stay would turn into a living arrangement that lasted two and a half years.

Gail and I had a lot in common. We had both been raised Catholic and our unconscious minds had been programmed the same way— we saw ourselves as good little Catholic girls who were gonna stay married forever. But both of our husbands decided they didn't want to be married anymore, and so here we were, two single mothers, dazed, confused, and in a fog. We had followed the rules—why were we not happy? Gail and I spent the next couple of years sorting out a lot of things together.

After we moved in, I soon began to look for a permanent place to live. After a few weeks, Gail said, "Please don't leave. I've never had so much freedom!" Having me in the house meant someone to help take care of her kids, someone to share cooking and gardening, and someone to share day-to-day life. She loved having me there, and I loved being there. So we stayed.

It was an important chapter in my life and the life of my son, too. Gail was sort of a hippie at heart, a northern California girl with a communal attitude. The theme of her home was "This is family property." Everything was shared—and Gail was in charge of the collective. If one kid needed an article of clothing and another kid had it, Gail simply "reallocated" the item to the kid who needed it. No questions asked. That's just the way things went in that household—my kid and her kids alike. It was perfect socialism, with Gail as the benevolent dictator. "Everybody owns everything" was her philosophy.

Gail and I gardened together, talking back and forth as we worked in the soil. We both needed time to heal from our divorces, time to sort out the confusion, time to get some clarity on the past and some focus on the future. It was an important chapter in each of our lives. Over time, I grew to realize how strong I really was, how even-tempered, and how I really could get my act together and go on with my life.

Gail was also an important influence on my son Sutton, giving him a tremendous creative bequest. He still considers Gail's house to be one of his homes. I see lingering qualities in him from our experience of living with Gail. She gave him complete artistic freedom, buying him a set of drums to encourage his music. Today Sutton is like a young hippie—broad-minded with a "live and let live" attitude.

Gail's generosity was more than anyone could ever ask or expect from a friend. She gave me a safe haven in which to mourn and heal and grow into the next chapter of my life. She gave my son a wonderful extended family in which to learn valuable lessons about sharing, community, and creativity. She showed her love for us in countless ways. I am eternally grateful to have a friend like Gail.

—Julie Ann Hill

It is the friends you can call up at 4 A.M. that matter.
—Marlene Dietrich, German actress

There are homes you run from and homes you run to.
—Laura Cunningham, playwright

GENEROUS: *What's in a Word?*

Giving with no strings attached

Expecting nothing in return

Noticing what others need and want

Exercising your imagination and creativity in giving

Realizing that "what goes around, comes around"

Opening your home as well as your heart

Understanding that it is the *giver* who is most
enriched

Sharing your time, attention, energy, money, and
love

Friendship Knows No Borders

IT WAS THE 1970S and the Pinochet coup in Chile triggered a mass exodus of many of that country's intellectuals. Practically the entire math department at the University of Chile came to Miami, where I was living at the time. Lumi was a member of this Chilean Diaspora who found their way to the United States to escape personal and professional persecution. Lumi and I met at the university and become fast friends.

In 1979 I moved to Cambridge, largely to help with the Chilean resistance movement there. Lumi and I stayed in touch by phone and by mail. We shared many of the things that young women share with one another—our young children, my romances (as a single mom) with Latin American men, career ups and downs, our hopes, our dreams, the stuff of our lives.

By the early '80s, Lumi (still in Miami) felt the stress of exile. Her baby had become a toddler. We were talking on the phone one day, and she confided in me that her husband had hit her. "Why don't you just pack up and get out of there? Come up here and stay with me," I told her. I had a big old Victorian house with plenty of room. Soon after, she and her daughter were living with me.

A couple of years later, Lumi and her toddler moved to Brazil. It was harder to stay in touch because international phone calls were terribly expensive in those days, and people often neglect to write letters—we all have such busy lives! Lumi and I lost touch. But I never stopped thinking about her and wondering how she was faring.

Thank goodness for the advent of the Internet! About five years ago, I was able to find her again and reestablish contact. Her daughter is now in her late twenties and a mother herself—so Lumi is a grandmother! Hard to believe—it seems like just yesterday, and we were so young.

Lumi lives in Rio now, where she works as a trilingual translator (Portuguese, Spanish, and English). She continues her social justice work as well. She e-mails amazing stories of her life, her thoughts on everything from the politics of women's rights to the philosophy of our relations with men from different cultures. Just like we did thirty years ago, we share our thoughts and feelings, woman to woman, friend to friend. Our e-mail conversations are heartfelt, deep, and intimate. Her second husband, a younger Argentine, just left her recently, so she is adjusting to being single again, and coincidentally I am dating younger European men, so, as ever, we have plenty to discuss.

You know, I have a sister who is thirteen years younger than me, and who inhabits a different world. We are not close at all. I feel more like Lumi is my sister. Maybe it's the bond of Chile and Latin America, maybe it's our common commitment to addressing political injustice, maybe it's the unique power of women's friendships. I don't know. All I know is that time and distance have done nothing to diminish our sisterly love. Even after years of separation and no face-to-face contact, we just pick up right where we left off.

—Christine Vida

We make a living by what we get, we make a life by what we give.
—Winston Churchill, British Prime Minister

The first duty of love is to listen.
—Paul Tillich, German-born theologian

A Beautiful Act of Love and Intimacy

A HYSTERECTOMY IS SOMETHING that all women hope they will never have to face—but sooner or later, some of us find that our reproductive systems are severely distressed and the operation becomes necessary. Such was the case for me in 1985.

One evening, about a week before my surgery, I was with a group of men and women from the nudist group to which I belonged. I was telling some of the women about how nervous I was about the upcoming operation, and they were wonderfully supportive. I also told them that I really didn't want to have my pubic hair shaved in the hospital, and I asked them if they would do it for me. Of course they said Yes.

It was one of the most powerful, loving, amazing experiences of my life. These women made a beautiful ritual of this event: they arranged a nest of pillows in which I sat; they lit candles and incense; they draped my upper body in a beautiful, luxurious silk blouse; they put on some lovely soothing music; and they gathered around me in a circle, taking turns shaving me with soft, gentle, loving strokes of the razor. Then later that afternoon they gave me a wonderful, relaxing, full-body massage. I couldn't have asked for a more comforting way to prepare for surgery. True friends, indeed.

—*Ruth Gold*

The hardest of all is learning to be a well of affection, and not a fountain, to show them we love them, not when we feel like it, but when they do.
　　—Nan Fairbrother, author

Celebrate a Friend

Susyn: THE OCCASION WAS JOAN'S fiftieth birthday party. She had also just sold her successful business, and to celebrate, Joan and her husband invited twenty of their closest friends and family for a weekend celebration at a resort in Jamaica. What a wonderful treat!

I had planned to do something really special for Joan's birthday. I wanted to give her the best present in the world. But I was going through a divorce, was in the process of moving, and my life was chaotic. The days flew by and before I knew it, there was only one day before we were to leave for Jamaica. It was time to come up with an idea, and fast! I thought, "What do you give a woman who has everything? She has a great husband, wonderful kids and grandkids, terrific success in business, and all the material things anyone could want."

Then I got an idea to give her a book that told her why she was special. I had a couple of childhood photos of Joan, so I had them color copied at Kinko's and made a cover with them saying, *In Celebration of Joan's 50th Birthday*. Then on the inside pages I wrote various headings:

My Funniest Time with Joan Was . . .
The Thing I Love Most about Joan Is . . .
What I've Learned from Joan Is . . .
My Birthday Wish for Joan Is . . .

When we got to Jamaica, I quickly wrote instructions asking everyone to respond to the prompts at the top of the pages—or to add any words or drawings that captured what they wanted to express to Joan. "And make sure Joan doesn't see what you are doing!"

We had twenty-four hours to get this done, and I gently reminded people to "sign the celebration book" that was to be given to Joan on Saturday night when she actually turned fifty. Saturday night, after Joan blew out her birthday candles, I walked to the front of the room, took a deep breath, and feeling the room filled with love, I looked at Joan and said, "This gift we made for you is filled with love so *you can see who you are through the eyes of people who love you.*"

JOAN: I was too embarrassed to read the book in front of everyone at the party, so Sunday morning after the party, I sat on the beach reading the book. Tears rolled down my face as I read each of the entries. What an amazing experience. I was overwhelmed; I could hardly take it in. It was the perfect gift.

When Susyn came out to the beach and joined me, I looked at her and said, "Everybody in the world deserves one of these. Everyone should have the experience of seeing who they are through the eyes of people who love them." And with that statement, a new business was born. I bought the domain name *www.celebratesomebody.com* and designed an Internet site that anyone can use to create a celebration book and then invite family and friends to upload photos, write stories, and recall memories. Once everyone contributes, the book is printed and given as a gift to be treasured for a lifetime.

The site is a big hit! Who knew that day in Jamaica, that Susyn's loving gesture would make such a big difference—not only in my life, but in the lives of thousands of people who have created celebration books for their family and friends.

And then it went even further. In August 2003, I received an order from a woman who was making a celebration book for her husband, serving in the Army, whose tour of duty in Iraq had just been extended. As I printed the book to send it to her, I thought, "How wonderful it would be if every soldier, in harm's way, could receive this gift of love and recognition." So I bought another domain name, *www.celebrateahero.com*—a website through which soldiers' friends and families can make special celebration books via the Internet and then send them to the men and women serving in the armed forces.

Susyn gave me a priceless gift of love, a thoughtful gesture with a huge impact. I've been able to give similar gifts to thousands of people all over the world. It's a reminder never to underestimate the power of the little things you can do for a friend. Who knows where they might lead?

—*Susyn Reeve and Joan Breiner*

Do not save your loving speeches for your friends till they are dead. Do not write them on their tombstones; speak them rather now instead.
—Anna Cummins, author

7

True Friends

Comfort and support us through
struggles and disappointments

Trouble is a sieve through which we sift
our acquaintances. Those too big to pass
through are our friends.
—ARLENE FRANCIS, actress, talk-show host

Hitting the Wall

SOMETIMES GOOD FRIENDS show up in the most surprising places. One would expect to make friends in school, in college, at church, in sports activities, through hobbies, in neighborhoods, and at work. But I never expected to find a true friend so close to the top of a major Fortune 500 corporation.

His name is Jim Shaffer, and he was the chief financial officer at the Los Angeles Times, where I worked in the late '80s. My first two weeks with the company were spent in orientation, beginning with individual meetings with all the senior executives whose offices were in the Publisher's Suite. I was a few days into this orientation when I met with Jim in his office. He was warm and friendly, handsome and outgoing, his boyish good looks giving him the appearance of a twenty-something junior executive rather than a forty-something CFO. I liked him instantly.

He asked me how I liked my job so far, and I responded enthusiastically. "What's not to like? Smart people, important work, great pay and benefits, and a high status organization—what more could a girl want?"

He smiled knowingly and reached for a piece of paper. On it he drew something like a diminishing cosine curve: Morale on the vertical axis and time on the horizontal; morale starting very positive, then declining to negative before recovering to a lower positive.

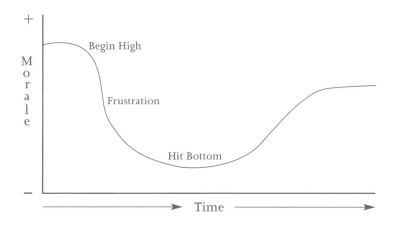

"Let me give you a little heads up," he said in a confidential tone of voice. "When you come in to the LA Times, you're excited, optimistic, full of energy and possibilities." He pointed to the top of the cosine curve. "Then when you've been here a while, you start running into obstacles. It isn't quite as wonderful as you initially thought." He points to the curve heading downward. "And it keeps getting worse, as you encounter the bureaucracy and get really frustrated. Finally, you hit bottom." He pointed to the bottom of the curve—then he circled it. "When you get there, call me. We'll have lunch."

"OK, thanks," I said, taking the paper with the curve on it. "I'll do that."

Several months went by, and sure enough, Jim was right. My experience was exactly the way he had predicted. Finally, I picked up the phone and told him, "I'm ready for that lunch."

We met for lunch the following week. "I wasn't expecting your call so soon," he began. "I thought I might hear from you in a year or a year and a half . . . but three months?"

"I'm a quick study," I replied unhappily. I poured out my tale of woe, alternating between tears and anger. I vented and railed—he listened. He nodded; he clucked; he shook his head sadly. He understood exactly what I was talking about. He was able to empathize and tell me I wasn't crazy. He was also able to help me see options and choices—I didn't have to be a victim of the bureaucracy of this stately old newspaper.

That was the beginning of a great friendship that is now nearly twenty years old. He coached me and counseled me several times during the five years that I spent at the paper. He commiserated with me, for he, too, had struggled with the glacial pace of work at this behemoth of a company. It was so hard to get anything done in such a calcified, ossified organization!

The biggest difference Jim made in my life was simply in his act of taking an interest. Having a senior executive take the time to support and encourage me made me feel valuable. It is so easy to feel lost and alone in an organization of more than 10,000 people, and Jim made me feel like someone was watching out for me. I needed to know that someone sincerely cared about me, and Jim provided exactly that.

He has since left the LA Times and moved on to be president of the Chicago Sun Times, and then president of Guy Gannett

Publishing. And I've since moved on to be a consultant, speaker, and author. But our friendship persists—across organizations, across the country, and across the years. I'll always be grateful for his friendship, and the difference he made in my life and my career.

What do we live for, if it is not to make life less difficult for each other.

—George Eliot (Mary Ann Evans), English writer

If you have made mistakes, even serious ones, there is always another chance for you. What we call failure is not the falling down but the staying down.

—Mary Pickford, silent-film star

STRUGGLE: *What's in a Word?*

See obstacles as temporary, not permanent.

Try many different approaches.

Rally friends and supporters to help.

Understand that struggles make us stronger.

Give yourself time to rest and regroup occasionally.

Gather the resources you need to prevail.

Let go of limiting beliefs.

Enjoy and celebrate your progress, no matter how
    slow or sporadic.

Rallying

WHEN MY HUSBAND OF seventeen years left me, I was devastated. My friends rallied 'round and supported in me so many creative ways. I don't know what I would have done without them! Here are some of the ways they helped me while I healed:

- Stayed with me the first week and helped me move every single picture on the walls down seven inches—to my eye level, not his.
- Ripped up the carpet in the bedroom, revealing nearly pristine wood floors. (The college friend who did this was ready to go out and rent a sander, if need be.)
- Tore down the sappy bathroom wallpaper with me and helped me sponge paint it in bright pink and yellow.
- Painted my kitchen red and white.
- Invited me to dinner—a lot.
- Hired someone to clean my house.
- One friend took me away for a weekend and went horseback riding on the beach because I wanted to, even though she was terrified of horses.
- A group of friends insisted I carry on the tradition of holiday dinners. I said I couldn't do it without my husband's help. They all pitched in instead. I found out it was about being together, not about all that I'd cooked and served.
- Mowed my lawn and cut down a dead tree in the backyard.

Every day I am thankful for my fabulous friends!

Nothing, I am sure, calls forth the faculties so much
as being obliged to struggle with the world.
      —Mary Wollstonecraft, British feminist, author

Foul Weather Friends

I'VE HEARD OF "FAIR WEATHER FRIENDS"—those who only like you when things are going fine and desert you when you hit hard times. But I came to realize that there are also "foul weather friends"—those who do just the opposite: hang out with you and commiserate when things are tough (misery does love company, I guess) and turn on you when you hit good times. Ouch, does that hurt!

Years ago, I was working at a university, developing continuing education programs for adults. I was new to the job and worked hard to achieve results, please my boss, and make money for the university. All of my coworkers seemed to like me, and several of us would often lunch together or have drinks at the faculty center pub after work.

My second semester in the job was terrific—there were huge enrollments in the classes I developed and my budgets were nice and fat as a result. I was feeling great about my success, and pleased that I had proven I could do the job well.

Then one day I heard disturbing gossip through the office grapevine: it was rumored that my job success happened because I was sleeping with various prominent professors on campus. I was hurt and confused. (Never mind that I was deeply in love with the man I was going to marry.) Why were several of my coworkers saying such mean and untrue things about me behind my back? I asked my office mate, Alan.

He shrugged as he said simply, "You make them look bad."

"What?!" I asked, incredulous.

"They've been on the job a long time, and you just came a year ago. Now you're outperforming them and it makes them look bad by comparison," he explained.

"But I thought we were friends," I objected.

"Well, I guess you know who your true friends are now, don't you?" he replied.

Alan was so helpful—he taught me to develop thicker skin. There have been subsequent times when people have been jealous or resentful, and Alan encouraged me not to take it personally. Their behavior speaks volumes about who *they* are—but it really has nothing to do with me. It's best just to ignore others' gossip and back-biting.

Alan was a true friend, as well as a great coworker. We shared an office and spent a lot of time together. I loved having him around, because he was really good at his job, and it made me want to be better at my job too. It was healthy competition—much as a tennis player loves to play with someone a little better than herself so that she rises to the occasion and becomes a better player.

I learned that my true friends are those who love me when I'm on top of the world, as well as while I'm climbing to get there. And my true friends help ease the disappointment caused by those who are only foul weather friends.

It is in the character of very few men to honor without envy a friend who has prospered.
—Aeschylus, Greek tragedian

Nothing changes your opinion of a friend as surely as success—yours or his.
—Franklin P. Jones, American businessman

In prosperity our friends know us; in adversity we know our friends.
—John Churton Collins, British literary critic

Life Is about Progress, Not Perfection

MY FRIEND KAREN CUTTS gave this advice to me one day when I was having trouble following a healthy plan of eating: "Don't let what you *can't* do stop you from what you *can* do."

I can't tell you how helpful those words were, not just regarding getting in shape, but in dealing with life as well. For many years, I was an "all or nothing" person. If I slipped a little bit on my food plan, I would think to myself, "Oh well, you've blown it now. Might as well eat what you want and start over again in the morning." I would use a little mistake to give myself permission to go whole hog. This extended to other areas of my life as well. They have a name for this kind of thinking—it's called perfectionism.

Karen taught me that progress in most any aspect of life is about evolution, not revolution. It's about doing 100 things 1% better, not doing one thing 100% better. It's learning that anything worth doing is worth doing badly at first.

Today, each meal in which I eat healthy food is one less meal of junk food. Each time I clean one room in my house, I am that much closer to having a clean house—I don't have to wait until I have time to clean the whole thing at once. And writing a rough first draft of a chapter is far superior to writing nothing at all, even if I don't have the time to do it perfectly. Karen taught me that life is about progress, not perfection.

> *Surviving means being born over and over.*
> —Erica Jong, writer

Knoc, Knoc . . . Who's There
When You Need Her?

IT WAS WHAT THEY CALL in Hollywood a "cute meet." I was out with friends one Friday night—we'd gone to a postmodern Japanese sake bar called Knoc Knoc. It was my favorite place in town, the place where I'd met my soul mate boyfriend, Robert. He was there with me that night, along with my friend Ursula. I was having a great old time, knocking back a few sakes in the lively ambience of the bar, which looked like the inside of an airplane. I turned to look at a piece of art that looked like a defused bomb, when I caught sight of Leslie Rossman.

Leslie was a coworker at the publishing house where I worked, but we hadn't met yet. I'd heard a lot about her—she was this hot young publicist from New York who'd been hired by HarperSanFrancisco to heat things up on the publicity front for our books. We'd been going through enormous change at the company, recently purchased by Rupert Murdoch, the Australian press baron. We never knew what new changes were going to be announced when we showed up for work each day, and the 250 employees there were pretty much shell-shocked. We had plenty to drink about.

When I spotted Leslie at Knoc Knoc, I made my way through the crowd, and when I got close enough, I semi-shouted over the noise, "Hey, aren't you Leslie Rossman—the hot new publicist from New York?" She was not amused. Here was this sake-soaked coworker accosting her on a Friday night, when she was just trying to relax like everyone else.

But somehow we made it through the initial off-putting moments and struck up a conversation. You couldn't imagine two more opposite personalities: her the intense, Jewish, brunette, petite New Yorker, and me the blonde, bosomy, peace-love-rock-and-roll California chick. But perhaps what they say about opposites attracting is true, and that night was born a best friendship.

I was her first real friend in San Francisco, and in subsequent months I took her around, showing her the lay of the land and introducing her to the city scene and my friends. We thoroughly enjoyed each other's company, and those early years of our friendship were sweet and fun-filled.

Then tragedy struck about a year later. Robert and I broke up, and I was devastated. Catatonic would be more accurate. I couldn't eat, I couldn't sleep, I couldn't function, and I had nowhere to go. Robert and I had been living together, and I had no idea where to go or what to do from moment to moment.

But Leslie knew. She turned into my Jewish mother, came over to my place, packed up my stuff, and took me back to her apartment. She fed me, drove me to work each day, consoled me while I cried, and took care of me in every way. I am sure that she saved my life. If it hadn't been for Leslie, I'm not sure I'd be alive today. I was such a mess, who knows what would have happened to me?

Thanks, Leslie. You still are the hot young publicist from New York . . . and aren't I lucky to have you as my best friend!?

—*Brenda Knight*

Friendship is certainly the finest balm for the pangs of disappointed love.

　　　　—Jane Austen, English novelist

Endings

IN 2000, MY HUSBAND, who meant all things to me, passed away suddenly after suffering a major heart attack while jogging. The life I knew and loved changed in an instant, and I was devastated. As strong as I thought I was and had always been, I didn't have the strength to deal with what was before me now.

My friends stepped in and took charge of me and my life and refused to allow me to succumb to depression. They became active members in my healing. They cried with me, recounted memories with me, and laughed with me. They helped me to understand the beauty and passion that I was blessed to have in my life with my husband and how so many people seek and never find it in their lifetime.

My friends helped me accept this involuntary new life that I had been given with renewed joy.

—Deborah Charles

The world is round, and the place which may seem like the end may also be the beginning.

—Ivy Baker Priest, U. S. treasurer during Eisenhower administration

Hardly Homeless

Children are gone,

Youth is gone,

Money is gone,

Home is gone,

My husband is gone!

Is there anything left?

I celebrate my fiftieth with my female friends.

No wonder I am in shock!

I have my eternal soul,

I have a choice to not blame,

A choice to not pity myself,

A choice to hope and trust.

Truly, my home is where I hang my hat,

My home is where my heart is.

Sharing a home for many years in the wealthiest county

in the nation,

Rarely missing a day of work,

I am—hardly homeless!

Thank you—Infinite—very much!

—Phyllis Woodward

Commitment is emotional intent backed up by action. Commitment isn't something you pledge, it's something you do. When they are there beside you, doing all the right things at the right time in the right way, their commitment will be obvious to you.
—Anthea Paul, Australian author

True Friends

Forgive us when we hurt them . . .
just as we forgive them

Love is an act of endless forgiveness,
a tender look which becomes a habit.
—PETER USTINOV, English actor, writer

Can You Keep a Secret?

MY FRIEND SHERRY was so excited. She had landed a new job as publisher of a small east coast paper in a national newspaper chain. She happily shared her good news with me, and asked that I keep it a secret. The current publisher at that paper was still on the job, and he didn't know he was being replaced. "Of course I'll keep your secret," I assured her. "Besides, who would I tell?" I had left the newspaper business a couple years earlier and was now conducting automotive training seminars for one of Detroit's Big Three manufacturers.

Shortly after Sherry told me her good news, I was in Maryland conducting seminars with my training buddy Paul. We drove to Annapolis to find someplace interesting to have dinner. During the course of the conversation that evening, we were talking about east coast versus west coast, comparing the pros and cons of each. I talked about how many of my west coast friends were relocating east, and wondered if I might move there myself. "In fact, my good friend Sherry just got a job on the East Coast and is moving here soon," I said to Paul. I told him briefly about her new job, thinking to myself, "Well, it's OK to tell Paul—he isn't in the newspaper business—he's in the training business. Sherry and Paul don't know any of the same people. It won't hurt to tell him." The conversation moved on, and that was the end of that.

A couple weeks later, I received a sheepish phone call from Paul. "You're not going to believe what happened," he began. I could tell by the tone of his voice that this was bad news. "I went to a local Chamber of Commerce breakfast here yesterday, and the guest speaker was a woman who is the regional vice president for that newspaper chain you and I were talking about. She gave an interesting presentation about the media and current events—she was just great. So afterward I went up to shake her hand and thank her for her presentation. I mentioned that I knew that the local paper was about to get a new publisher, your friend Sherry. Well, she suddenly turned cool and replied, 'No, that's not correct. That paper already has a publisher.' I knew instantly that I had screwed up—obviously this was something I wasn't supposed to know. So I backed off, apologized, and left. But I figured I better call you, because I let the cat out of the bag."

"Oh god," I groaned. I couldn't believe what he told me. What were the chances of Paul crossing paths with Sherry's new boss? I was stunned and mortified. My friend had asked me to keep her secret, and what had I done? Blabbed it to another friend. And now Sherry would be in trouble with her boss for not keeping the new job secret.

I had created a royal mess with my indiscretion!

"Well, it's not your fault, Paul," I told him. "I didn't tell you that it was a secret. It never occurred to me that you would repeat it—much less to someone in the newspaper business! Jeez, this is awful."

"I'm so sorry," he said. "Is there anything I can do?"

"Yeah, shoot me," I replied.

I got off the phone and called Sherry immediately. I hoped that I had gotten to her before her new boss did. I told her what had happened, and waited for her to yell at me. She had every right to yell, and more.

She was horrified at my tale, but she didn't yell. "Well, I learned an important lesson here," she said. "If I want my secret to stay a secret, I can't tell *anybody*."

"I learned an important lesson, too," I replied. "When someone asks me to keep something a secret, I need to do just that. There is no such thing as a 'safe' person to tell. I violated your confidence, and I am so sorry. I blew it. Can you ever forgive me? Can I make it up to you somehow?"

"Of course, I forgive you," she said. "But I can't worry about you right now—I have to call my new boss and clean this up with her. She's gonna think I'm very unprofessional, sharing confidential personnel information with someone else. She might rescind the job offer. I don't know what she'll do. You and I can talk later, but I have to take care of this mess right now."

We got off the phone, and I felt just terrible. What kind of a friend was I, creating such a huge problem for my friend? I wouldn't blame her if she didn't want to be friends any more.

But Sherry was a true friend, and she forgave me. In this experience we both saw how easy it is to break a confidence, sharing it with someone you trust, thinking in all sincerity that you hadn't really broken the confidence at all, since it was a trusted friend.

Sherry broke her boss's confidence by telling me, and I broke Sherry's confidence by telling Paul. It was a daisy-chain of secret-sharing that created a big mess for all of us. It was a painful lesson, one I'll never forget.

Today when someone asks me, "Can you keep a secret?" I answer, "I'd rather not." Secrets are a dangerous burden I'd rather not carry. And forgiveness is something I'd like to ask for a little less often!

P.S. Sherry still got the job.

*It is **very easy** to forgive others their mistakes; it takes more grit and gumption to forgive them for having witnessed your own.*
—Jessamyn West, Quaker author

Getting Rid of Old Baggage

Holding on to resentments is like swallowing poison and hoping the other person will die. In carrying around old baggage, the person I hurt the most is myself. If I want to live my life happy, joyous, and free, I must find a way to drop that baggage and resolve any unfinished business that's cluttering up my life and clogging up my heart. How can I do that? Here are a few ways:

- Write a letter pouring out all my grievances, read it to a trusted friend, then burn it—letting the resentments go up in smoke.
- Call the person I resent and apologize for <I>my<I> part in our problem.
- Pray for the other person every day for three weeks. Look at ways in which others might resent me and take steps to make amends to clear them up.
- Just let it go. Sometimes it's as simple as that. Make a decision to free myself from the corrosive burden of angry resentment.

Don't get bitter . . . get better!

—Anthea Paul, Australian author

She Said/She Said

ELISABETTA AND I were great friends for many years. We had met in our senior year at high school in South Africa, and although we were so different we became incredibly close. Over the next few years we did almost everything together and laughed and talked *all* the time. I skipped work to audit her anthropology classes at the university. We danced until dawn at discos all over town, flirting outrageously with all the guys—but we always left parties together and would compare notes after.

Once we were sitting on the floor of her small apartment laughing about how we would be old and grey, married and divorced a few times and still sitting together, laughing and sharing stories.

She was great—smart, funny, charming, a great conversationalist . . . and a little bit flaky. You know how some people seem a tad unreliable, or inconsistent? Well, that was part of Elisabetta too.

About twenty years ago I left South Africa and moved to the United States with my husband Jonathan. Elisabetta and I kept in touch by phone and by letter (e-mail wasn't yet invented), continuing our friendship long distance.

One day I called her because I was having some problems with my extended family. She knew my history with them, and I needed help. I asked her advice. She said she'd give it some thought and then write to me.

Weeks went by, and I eagerly awaited her post. Nothing came. Weeks turned into months, and my disappointment turned to anger.

"Such a flake!" I thought to myself. I wrote her a letter telling her how hurt I was that she had not followed through on her commitment to me. I worded it carefully, holding out hope that she would see her mistake, own up to it, and make things right. But she didn't. I never got an answer to that letter.

Years went by, and I thought I was done with our friendship. But somehow, she was still in my mind and I missed her. It became clear to me that I still needed to get some closure on our friendship—we had unfinished business with each other.

In 1997, I went back to South Africa to visit my family. I also felt I really needed to speak to Elisabetta. The day after I arrived I looked her up in the phone book and called her. She was so happy to hear from me, it was like no time had passed. We had that same old happy chemistry that we had always experienced. On the phone she suggested we go to Kruger Park for a long weekend—which she knew I loved, but then said, "I suppose we should get together first and see if we even want to spend that amount of time together." We agreed to meet for lunch or tea first.

She came to pick me up, and it was like we had seen each other the day before. Our lunch seemed to fly by, and we were not aware of anyone else. I told her about my hurt and confusion and asked why she hadn't replied to my letter. I explained that in the letter I had very carefully left the door open so that we could still save our friendship. But that wasn't how it read to Elisabetta—to her, the letter seemed to end the relationship, so there was no point in responding. It was one of those classic things like you read about in novels or see in the movies: I intended one thing, but she perceived just the opposite. There was a big gap between intent and impact.

That conversation was all it took to get our friendship back on track. There were no accusations or recriminations, no guilt or apologies—in the course of our talk that afternoon, our conflict seemed to dissipate, vaporize into thin air. We both just let it go. I guess we both realized that our friendship was too big and too important to be ended over a misunderstanding and miscommunication. True friendship can overcome small hurts and perceived slights. Just like a marriage, a true friendship involves tolerance, forgiveness, perspective, patience, grace, and tact, and giving the other the benefit of the doubt.

Elisabetta and I both learned an important lesson in friendship: Don't sweat the small stuff . . . (and life is mostly small stuff!).

—*Beverley Davimes*

What I cannot love, I overlook. Is that friendship?
—Anaïs Nin, French-born novelist, diarist

Let us take note of our own faults and leave others' alone.
—Teresa of Avila, Spanish Carmelite nun, mystic, saint

Infidelity

AMY HAD BEEN MY LIFELONG best friend. We were little girls together and had grown up together. In the '70s we got into the party scene together in a big way. It was a wild time, to be sure.

One night, Amy was over at my apartment, and we were sitting around with my husband and some other friends, smoking, drinking, and listening to music. I was tired and a little high, so I headed off to bed before midnight. I don't know what time everyone else left—I was dead to the world. But Amy and my husband were very much alive, and in the wee small hours of the morning, they had sex together. She was gone by the time I got up the next morning, so I was none the wiser.

Many years passed, about fifteen years, I think. My husband and I had long since split, and Amy and I were still best friends. One day she told me about that fateful night. The guilt had been haunting her all those years, and tears poured out profusely as she confessed and asked my forgiveness.

I was shocked and hurt. How could my best friend commit adultery with my husband? Yes, I was loaded, and so were they, but that's no excuse. I didn't speak to her for months.

As I nursed my hurt pride, I realized that our years and years of friendship far outweighed one night of inebriated indiscretion. I found room in my heart to forgive her.

Amy and I got through the crisis, and we're still best friends today.

—*Maria Stassinopoulos*

Forgiveness is the act of admitting we are like other people.
  —Christina Baldwin, author, speaker

How life catches up with us and teaches us to love and forgive each other.
  —Judy Collins, folk singer

Keeping Commitments

MY FRIEND SUZANNE was a terrific friend in many respects, but she had one really bad habit. We would make plans to meet for lunch or dinner, and often she would call up the day of our planned meeting and cancel. Now, everybody has to do this once in a while. Things come up, I know. But with Suzanne, it was a regular thing.

Once, after Suzanne cancelled on me for the sixth time in a row, I had to do something. I was so angry with her, and I knew that I couldn't be friends with someone who continued to stand me up at the last minute.

I called her and asked her about her cancellation habit: "This is the sixth time in a row that you've cancelled at the last minute. I need to know, Suzanne. Did you get a better offer; did you not look in your appointment book until today; or are you simply a flake?"

She was very apologetic and admitted that she did not look in her appointment book when she made our lunch plans. When the day arrived, she saw she had a previous engagement, and cancelled. She admitted that this was a habit—poor time management.

I explained that it didn't work for me, and I told her how I felt when she repeatedly cancelled. She apologized; I accepted.

Our friendship since then is much closer . . . and she doesn't cancel our dates anymore. I think that working through a conflict or problem in a friendship actually makes the relationship stronger. Apologies and forgiveness are powerful tools. We should all use them more often.

—Kitty Cole

If it's very painful for you to criticize your friends—
you're safe doing it. But if you take the slightest
pleasure in it, that's the time to hold your tongue.
—Alice Duer Miller, poet, playwright

You cannot shake hands with a clenched fist.
—Indira Gandhi, Prime Minister of India

How Do You Forgive?

Feel your hurt.

Open your mind.

Release your anger.

Give love a chance.

Inquire within your heart.

Venture into dialogue.

Embrace the other person.

Nudge yourself to keep at it, even when you
   don't want to.

Enjoy new possibilities and freedom.

Seek Divine guidance and help.

Savor your new serenity and peace.

Misunderstanding

CATHY AND I MET in Guam way back in 1982—I was her sponsor in the Navy, and it was my job to welcome her and her husband to the base and to help them get acclimated to our base and the local culture. We've been good friends ever since. It's the kind of friendship where we may not see each other for long stretches—years sometimes—but when we do see each other, we just pick up right where we left off. Perhaps military friendships are like that, I don't know. I just know that ours was.

In 1990, Cathy received orders to ship out to the Middle East to participate in Operation Desert Storm. At the time, I was working in the Defense Intelligence Agency (DIA) in Arlington, Virginia, and because of my high-level security clearance, my superiors determined that I was needed there and would not be going overseas.

I drove Cathy to the airport in Philadelphia—it was April. She was flying out to meet her ship, the USS *Santa Barbara*. This overseas assignment was costing her dearly—she was in the process of a divorce, and because she was leaving the country, she lost custody of her kids. That's the way things were in those days—it was terrible.

We were both so tense in the car on the way to the airport. We got into a huge argument about the fat content in McDonald's hamburgers! I think neither one of us knew how to deal with our feelings that day. It was an unhappy parting.

A few years later, we saw each other again and had an opportunity to talk about that day. "I thought you were jealous," she told me. "You always got the exciting assignments and got to go to exotic places. I thought you were jealous that I was going to participate in Desert Storm and you weren't."

"No, I felt guilty because you were going and I wasn't. I'm single and it would have been easy for me to go, but you were a mother with young kids, and it wasn't fair that you lost your kids over this," I replied.

We looked at one another with mixed feelings of sadness and happiness. Sadness that we had let this misunderstanding fester for so long, happiness that we had finally talked about it and resolved it.

We're both retired now and continue to be fast friends, though we live in different parts of the country. Our friendship has withstood the test of time and distance . . . and misunderstanding.

—*Sharon Williams*

Forget injuries; never forget kindnesses.
—Confucius, Chinese philosopher

Forgiveness is the key to action and freedom.
—Hannah Arendt, philosopher

True Friends

Let us love them back

Love is, above all, the gift of oneself.
—Jean Anouilh, French dramatist

I Would Gladly Pay Ransom for My Friends

WHEN I WAS IN HIGH SCHOOL, my girlfriends and I would send each other "ransom letters" when we were having boyfriend problems or some other typical teenage difficulty. We called them ransom letters because they were like the letters kidnappers would send to the families of their victims—made up of words and phrases cut from magazines and newspapers, and pasted together on sheets of paper—demanding a ransom for the safe return of the kidnap victim. My girlfriends and I composed our own ransom letters to one another—not out of fear that someone would recognize our handwriting, but because it captured our imagination and seemed more fun than just a regular written note.

As I got older, I would assemble "ransom books" for friends when they were going through some personal crisis. I also made ransom books for my kids on special occasions—birthdays, graduations, holidays. When my best friend got married, I gave her a personal ransom book at her bridal shower—and when all the women at the shower read it, they just loved it. Everyone I've ever given one of these books to is delighted. The personal touch means so much—it tells my friends that I care about them enough to make them something special—just for them—like no other in the world. Each book is as unique as its recipient.

I've spent many years collecting clippings, phrases, paragraphs, words, metaphors, snippets of commentary from magazines, books, and newspapers. This vast assortment of words and phrases forms a sort of collective consciousness of the women and men who originally wrote them. In taking the words out of the mouths (rather, out of the pens and laptops) of others, and putting them together in new patterns and paragraphs, I like to think I'm tapping into that vast collective consciousness to express the inexpressable—friendship, companionship, love, courage, compassion, hope, and joy.

The words and phrases I clip from magazines form a chorus of voices—singing of love and life, turning points and dead ends, holidays and holy days, menarche and menopause, children and parents, boyfriends and husbands, and much, much more. I invite the recipient of each book to read, reflect, recollect and re-collect, reframe, rejoice, and remember her own life.

Each book is one of a kind, compiled with a particular person in mind. Some of them are happy and funny. Some are more serious and philosophical. All of them are filled with love. It's my own special way of loving back the people who have loved me.

—*Marsha Karzmer*

Remember, the greatest gift is not found in a store or under a tree, but in the hearts of true friends.
—Cindy Lew, author

What Goes Around, Comes Around

THIS PAST SUMMER I was invited to be part of the Los Angeles Mart, Artists Colony for eight days. I had no idea how I was going to manage taking care of all of my household daily activities during this time. The first night I came home from a ten-hour day, I was greeted by clean dishes and a lovely dinner prepared for me. The second night, all of my laundry had been done, the space was cleaned, and dinner was ordered in for me. And it went on like that for the entire eight days of the show!

I asked my friend Ralph, who was staying with me, and my partner, Jack, how they could have known. They just said, "You always take care of everyone else, now it is your turn to be taken care of!" Of course, I cried like a fool when they said that. Talk about a real vacation without leaving home!

—Jaye Alison Moscarello

Friends are the family we choose for ourselves.
—Sandra Magsamen, artist, author

Teaching Others How to Give

DONNA WAS A GIVER, a caretaker, someone who was always going out of her way to help others. In her mid-forties, Donna was a remarkably generous person, and I loved her dearly. She was my best friend. We lived near each other in San Francisco and often went to movies, parties, plays, and other things together.

I started working several days a week in San Diego. One day I called Donna while I was away, and I could hear something different in her voice. She said simply, "I've been diagnosed with cancer." Those are words you never want to hear from your best friend . . . or from anyone, for that matter. I was in shock. Her next words would change my life forever, opening a new dimension of experience that I could never have anticipated. "I have to go to the doctor in a few days to get the results of my MRI, and I don't want to go alone. Would you go with me?" she asked.

Her request was nothing short of remarkable . . . and an enormous gift. It was the beginning of a process in which she taught me how to ask for help, how to receive with grace and dignity, and how to bring together the people who love you when you need them most. Donna knew that she wanted people around her—that no matter what the future held, she did not want to go through this alone. Over the next few months, I watched her as she gently organized her friends into a loose but effective support system.

There were eight of us in the core group, and we had a meeting (without Donna present) to discuss what we could do and what we couldn't. We talked about how we felt about her illness—our own emotions and feelings. We made commitments in whatever way we could to provide what Donna needed. In the beginning, she needed three primary things: to get to work, to get out to social activities, and to get to doctors' appointments. She also needed us to spread the word and tell her other friends, to save her from the emotional and physical drain of having to explain her illness again and again.

We took shifts helping Donna. Since I was away for part of each week, I had the evening role, with a tuck-in call to her every night to see how she was doing as she went to bed. Others had morning duties, afternoon commitments. So in our core group we didn't see each other much, but we didn't need to. We were a virtual support team, like ships passing in the night, each of us committed to the same goal—to be there to give Donna whatever she needed from us.

As time went on, her needs changed and grew. More people pitched in and helped out in various ways—cooking, cleaning, helping with medical care. In the final month of Donna's life, a relative of hers came to stay . . . and so did my cat. Donna had always loved my cat, and she asked if he could come and be with her. Of course, I said "Yes." He was a sweet, affectionate guy, and I'm sure he didn't mind being loaned to my dying friend.

The fact that she could ask for what she needed and wanted continued to impress me. She made it so much easier for us—for all of her friends. She recognized that good friends always want to help, but they often don't know how. It is such an awkward situation . . . your friend has six months to live and you don't know what to say or do. Sometimes people just disappear when their friends are ill or dying because they can't handle their own awkwardness. Donna solved that problem for us. She didn't wait for people to offer their help, or ask what they could do. She knew what she needed, and she took the initiative to ask us to help her. What remarkable courage! What remarkable grace and poise in a terrible situation!

I learned so much from my experience with Donna's illness and death. She was a role model and inspiration. With all that Donna taught me, I started the SafetyNet Project, for people who need support and assistance going through not just illness, but other traumatic situations as well. I've developed a seminar and a workbook for teaching people how to support their friends in times of trouble. It is my tribute to the wisdom and courage of Donna, and the way she enriched my life, and the lives of all her friends, as she taught us how to die in the loving arms of her community of friends. She gave us all the opportunity to give back to her. After all her years of being a giver, her final act of true friendship was teaching us how to receive.

For further information about the SafetyNet Project, contact Susan Belgard at *sbelgard@comcast.net*

—*Susan Belgard*

I expect to pass through this world but once; any good thing therefore that I can do, or any kindness that I can show to any fellow creature, let me do it now; let me not defer or neglect it, for I shall not pass this way again.
—Etienne De Grellet, writer, philosopher

GIVING BACK: What's in a Word?

Going the extra mile

Involved in each other's lives

Vested interest in mutual well-being

Interested in helping out

Needing one another

Growing by giving

Being gracious and kind

Acknowledging one another's love

Communicating lovingly, honestly

Keeping commitments to one another

True friendships are not about give and take. . . .
They are about give and give.
  —Anonymous

Returning the Favor

FOLK WISDOM TELLS US that "it is better to give them receive." What it doesn't say is that it is also *easier* to give than to receive, at least for many of us. When we are giving, we are in control. We get to be the hero, the generous one, the thoughtful one, the one to whom others are grateful. It is actually harder to be the recipient, for in the receiving role, we are not in control; we are in the passive role of being receptive, and we often feel beholden to the person who is giving to us.

I've learned this firsthand with my cousin Marilyn Jensen, who is also a dear friend. She lives just around the corner and she is always doing thoughtful things for me: she picks up a case of cat food when she goes to Costco; she buys candles on sale and brings me some; best of all, she loves to cook (and I don't) and invites me over for dinner frequently. Sometimes I feel that our relationship is a little unbalanced—like I'm her poor country cousin, or something, and she takes pity on me and feeds me. Of course, that's not true; it just feels that way occasionally.

She's also been there for me when big things happen. The day I took a nosedive down a flight of stairs, dislocating my shoulder and fracturing my arm, she gave up her Sunday afternoon to follow the ambulance to the hospital and keep me distracted from the pain while we waited for the ER team to decide how they were going to treat my injuries. She then drove me home, stopping at the pharmacy to get the painkillers, fed me some soup and crackers before tucking me into bed. Marilyn is like the big sister I never had.

Her boyfriend, John Denney, has also been a wonderful friend to me. A retired cardiologist, he often answers my medical questions when I'm curious about something. He even made a house call to me in the middle of the night when I was ill with who-knows-what . . . and I thought I was having a heart attack. He showed up at the front door with stethoscope, thermometer, and blood pressure monitor in hand—an angel of mercy indeed!

Finally one day, I had the opportunity to return their many favors. Marilyn and John were flying in his ultralight plane and crashed into an avocado grove. Both were seriously injured, spending a few days in the hospital before they were brought home to recuperate. I made pharmacy runs for them, picking up their prescriptions; I went to Chinatown to pick up soft noodles, some yummy soup, and other things I thought they could eat; I made trips to the grocery store every couple of days to get whatever they felt like eating. And while I wasn't happy that Marilyn and John were injured, I *was* happy to have the opportunity to take care of them, after the many times they had taken care of me. I could drive them where they needed to go, call and see what they needed from the store, pick up the mail, haul out the trash cans on pick-up day, and other simple things like that.

That old folk saying is right—it *is* better to give than receive. But it's even better when you have the opportunity to do both!

SERVICE: *What's in a Word?*

Selflessness

Empathy

Reliability

Vitality

Integrity

Commitment

Expecting nothing in return

Strive to be the servant of all; for acting thus, you'll do more for yourself than others.

—Teresa of Avila, Spanish Carmelite nun, mystic, saint

Some people say, "Give till it hurts." I prefer to say, "Give till it feels good!"

—Rev. Ed Bacon, rector in Pasadena, CA

The Brother I Never Had

RICK WAS THE BROTHER I never had. We were both born in 1948 in Queens, New York; he was Italian and I'm Jewish, and we had instant simpatico the moment we met. He was an AIDS patient and I was his intravenous home-care nurse, making house calls twice a week to administer medication through a port-a-catheter in his chest. He was taking an enormous amount of medication—twenty-two oral medications daily, in addition to the IV and other meds. What impressed me most about Rick was his courage.

I had just gone back to school to earn my bachelor's degree in nursing and was feeling sorry for myself—married, with a full-time job, and going to school on top of it all. I thought it was more than I could handle. That is, until I met Rick. How could I complain about the burdens of my life when this guy was so courageous in the face of terminal illness? Rick taught me how to keep things in perspective.

We had so much fun together—he was smart, funny, irreverent, and kind. I had grown up with a twin sister as well as an older sister, but I'd always wanted a brother—Rick quickly became the brother I never had. I told him that once, and he quipped, "Sure, I'm the bar mitzvah you never got to go to!" We laughed. I always felt so comfortable in his presence, like we'd known each other all of our lives.

Rick had a wonderful cat named Boo-Boo—he had big green eyes and was very talkative. Boo didn't like other people much, but whenever I made my twice-weekly visits, Boo would be all over me, all over Rick's medical chart, all over everything. "I don't know why he does that," Rick would say. "He's not like that with anyone else—he must really like you."

I had lost my own cat a couple months earlier, and I was glad for this cat's affection. Rick shouldn't have had a cat at all at that point (he possessed two cats and a dog)—he was really too ill. But I couldn't bring myself to tell him that. All I could say was, "If it gets to the point that you can't take care of Boo-Boo anymore, I'll be happy to take care of him for you." Rick made that decision about a year later, and Boo came to live with me. He was an extension of Rick, in my mind, and I was happy to share my home with him. I sometimes called Boo-Boo by the name "Rickeedoodle," and when I did, Boo-Boo would always stop and look at me so strangely. I suspect it was the name "Rick" within it that he was so used to hearing.

I cared for Rick for almost two years. Toward the end, Rick kept trying to tell me that he was dying, but I didn't want to hear it. "You're doing fine," I would say to him whenever he said, "Wendie, I'm dying." Toward the very end he told me to keep my beeper on all the time, something I didn't want to do when I wasn't on duty. He also made me promise that I would "pronounce him" when the time of his death came (this involves taking pulse, blood pressure, and so on, and legally noting the time of death). Of course I said Yes.

One night I had a dream. It was dark and Rick and I were in the ocean, treading water. We weren't panicked or anything—we were just in the water, talking. I was facing toward shore and Rick was facing the deep water. "I came to say good-bye," he said. "It's time for me to go." I said, "Do you really have to go?" and he nodded Yes. We looked into each other's eyes and faces for awhile as we treaded water. Then we smiled at each other and I remember nodding to him that I accepted his decision. In my dream, I expected him to move on out to the deeper water, but he didn't. Instead, as I looked toward the shore, it became illuminated, and I saw crowds of people on the shore, all of them wearing long gowns. While we were still looking at each other, the tide pulled Rick toward the shore and he joined the people there. I just stayed where I was, in the dark water, watching him move away. I didn't move. Then I awoke. I looked at the clock; it was 3 A.M.

The next morning I told my husband about my dream. "Rick came to say good-bye to me," I said. It was about 8 A.M. and I was heading off to take care of another patient before I made my scheduled 9 A.M. visit to Rick. My beeper went off; it was Rick's number. I knew what the call was about. I returned the call and Rick's boyfriend answered. "I'll wait for you," he said. "Rick passed on in the night but he wanted you to pronounce him, so I'll wait till you get here."

I went to my first appointment and had a hard time controlling my tears. Then I went to Rick's house and did what I had promised to do. Despite the fact that he had been dead for hours, I had to go through the prescribed steps in pronouncing a death. I did everything I was supposed to do, called the coroner, called the Neptune

Society, and then broke down sobbing. I held his cold, gray body in my arms and just sobbed and sobbed. My brother was dead. Rick's boyfriend made me some tea, and we talked in between my nursing chores.

The memorial service was like nothing I had ever attended before. Rick was a Quaker, and the service was held in a Friends' meeting hall. His doctor was there, his minister, and at least a hundred friends, or more. It was so simple. People just spoke as the spirit moved them, one after another, telling stories about what Rick had meant to them. One lady sang a beautiful song for Rick (she sounded like Joan Baez). I learned a lot about Rick that day, as we often do when someone dies and we learn what that person had done and experienced in his life. The word that kept coming to my mind was *courage*.

I wanted to speak, too, but every time I thought I would stand up, I would choke up on tears. Finally, after about two hours of testimonials, I was able to speak. "You know," I began, "in taking care of Rick, I always thought I was Florence Nightingale. Here I was, on my errands of mercy, making visits to a dying man. But after listening to everyone speak here today, I see that Rick spent his dying days taking care of other people—helping them come to terms with his death, consoling them, joking with them, reassuring them. What I see now is that I wasn't Florence Nightingale—Rick was."

Many of the people at the Quaker memorial service, including myself, donated money to buy a memorial bench for Rick. A year later, this special bench was installed in Golden Gate Park in a favorite spot of Rick's. We had a wonderful ceremony. Rick's parents came, and a couple hundred of his friends. I was again impressed with the stories of how Rick had loved his friends and how they loved him back. What a remarkable man he was, and how lucky I was to have had him in my life—even for just two short years.

Boo-Boo lived for another ten years, and at the end, when his kidneys were shutting down, I infused him with fluids for several months to help keep him alive. I nursed him in his dying days, much as I had nursed Rick. That was four years ago, and I have been unable to get another cat until just recently. I've been mourning both Rick and Boo-Boo—my friend/brother and his wonderful cat.

I named my new cat Murray, after my father who passed away earlier this year. But both my husband and I alternate calling him Murray or Boo-Boo. Both Rick and Boo-Boo are alive and well in my memory. God bless them both. May they rest in peace.

—*Wendie Silverman-Martin*

It is not what you give your friend but what you are willing to give that determines the quality of the friendship.
— Mary Dixon Thayer, writer of poems and prayers for children

True Friends

Know the power of community. . . .
Together we can do almost anything!

Never doubt that a small group of
dedicated people can make a difference.
Indeed it is the only thing that ever has.
—MARGARET MEAD, anthropologist

Women "Exchanging Brains"
with One Another

ANITA GOLDSTEIN MOVED TO the Bay Area in the summer of 1995. A few months later, her friend Susan Goldstein said, "I have several friends whose lives are in transition. Why don't we invite them to do some brainstorming?" Anita, a woman whose idea of fun is to work with like-minded people setting things in motion, was delighted to be asked. They set a date and sent out the word to all their local friends.

"Our plan was to do this once or twice, to help our friends get a handle on how to think about their lives in a new way," Anita tells the story. "A the end of the first meeting, several people said, 'This is such valuable stuff—let's do it every month!' Susan and I looked at each other, shrugged our agreement, and it was a done deal. That was almost ten years ago, and we've been meeting ever since."

"We hadn't intended for the group to be all women," Susan elaborates. "We invited our partners, but they were busy that night. Once we'd experienced brainstorming with a group of women, it was clear that it was exactly what we wanted to be doing!"

"It's been a wonderful experience for us," Anita says. "I facilitate the meetings and Susan takes notes for the group while we brainstorm. Sometimes other members of the group help out with the note taking. That way, people don't have to take notes for themselves; they can just be present to the love, wisdom, humor, and generosity of the women in the room who are brainstorming their questions.

"Over the years we have brainstormed all kinds of questions—job and career issues, family dilemmas, business and marketing questions, intimate personal queries, spiritual concerns, and much, much more," Susan elaborates. "Nothing is off limits. We'll do our best with any question anyone wants to brainstorm."

And the results of all this female brainpower? "We could write a whole book about the amazing results that have come out of this process!" Anita replies. "Some women have found innovative ways to search for the men of their dreams; new career opportunities have opened up for others; websites have been built, businesses have been birthed; our members have navigated all sorts of life transitions with the help of the women who engage in the brainstorming process. Prayers and healing energy are offered for those who request them; travel tips are generated for some of our globe-trotting members; and business contacts of all kinds have been shared among the women. I could go on and on about the ways the Brain Exchange has brought about changes in people's lives."

"The Brain Exchange is about generous, bright, talented, creative women gathering to generate community," Susan summarizes. "The *process* is just as important as the results. Being together—talking, sharing, laughing, contributing, listening, giving and receiving—is valuable in and of itself. In some ways, the results—the actual brainstorms—are the icing on the cake. Humans are social creatures—we are meant to live and work in community."

Anita reaches for an article to read to me: "I saw this recently—it was part of an article in *Heifer* magazine that talked about how each of us *can* make a difference in the world. It struck me that it could easily be describing what the Brain Exchange is up to—networking and sharing resources."

- Albert-Lazlo Barabasi, a physicist, writes, "We have come to see that we live in a small world where everything is linked to everything else."
- Francis Lappé writes, "Networks are the key to understanding the world."
- Barbasi adds, "Small changes . . . affecting only a few of the nodes or links can open up hidden doors, allowing new possibilities to emerge."
- Lappé concludes, "If we think of our actions as 'entry points' (into the network of life), each affecting a node in the pattern, then we see that we are actually shifting the whole pattern when we act with clear intention. . . . What a sense of power!!" (*Heifer*, May/June 2004, *www.heifer.org*)

Anita and Susan look at me and smile. Women in community.

For further information about the Brain Exchange, visit *www.thebrainexchange.com*

Any two of us are smarter than any one of us.
—Wayne Paulson

A Woman's Wheels

CHRIS TIMMINS IS AN amazing woman. Twenty-six years ago, she and her husband were preparing to leave San Diego and move to Oregon. That bright, sunny morning while they were finishing up last-minute details, Chris was feeling nostalgic and decided to take one last spin around Fiesta Island in her beloved little BMW convertible. What happened to her on that drive is still a bit of a mystery—was it the hot sun, was it fatigue, what was it that caused her to black out while driving? She could feel herself losing consciousness and tried to pull over to the side of the road. But she lost control and crashed into a cement road divider. When she regained consciousness in the hospital, she was a quadriplegic. Her whole life was turned upside down.

Chris's husband left her about four years later. She lost her job as a schoolteacher and had to fight for the next year to get it back. She also spent the next two years battling with the state of California to get them to pay for a handicap van that would allow her to drive. Such a van cost $75,000 in those days—an impossible amount for a woman now alone who had just lost her life as she had known it.

Her health challenges weren't over, either. Many physicians won't treat quads because of their many special health concerns. Then, thirteen years later, Chris was struck with breast cancer.

Chris not only rose to meet each of these personal and professional crises, she triumphed over them. She was finally able to convince the San Diego School District that her presence in the classroom would greatly enrich the education of her students. Her message to the kids: "It's not the events of your life that determine the kind of future you'll have. It's how you respond to those events that gives you quality in your life." Chris was, and is, the living embodiment of that message.

Chris was able to get her special van from the state—her Freedom Van, which gave her the ability to go to work every day, and to be out and about like millions of other mobile southern Californians. And she found a physician, Dr. Donna Brooks, who would see to Chris's unique medical needs over the years.

I got to know Chris through Donna, and we've been friends for twenty-plus years. I've always been impressed with her pluck and optimism in the face of tragedies, struggles, and losses that would have done in a lesser woman.

Last year, Chris hit a final roadblock, and this one she just didn't know how to overcome. Her van was now twenty years old and just about worn out. The state program only provides one van per person in their lifetime. (I'm not sure why . . . maybe they don't expect disabled people to live so long?) And today, a specially equipped van for a person who has to drive with her head costs $115,000. How could a single woman, on a schoolteacher's salary, afford such an expensive vehicle? If she could no longer drive, she would have to quit her job, just seven years short of retirement. Chris had no idea what to do. For the first time, it seemed that this breaking-down hunk of metal was going to be the last straw that would do her in.

One day Chris and I were talking about her predicament. It seemed like such a dumb problem—after all she'd been through— this ancient van was going to stop her? I just couldn't accept that. "This is ridiculous," I told her. "We're just gonna get you a new van."

"But how?" Chris asked.

"Never mind how," I told her. "We're just going to go buy the van tomorrow and we'll figure out how to pay for it later!"

And so we did. We did some research and found that the van she needed had to be a 2003 model, because the 2004 model had a gas tank in it that would prohibit it from being modified for a handicapped-accessible vehicle. And we found that there were only seven such vans left in the entire state. So we found a dealer who had one, and we bought it. Our small private foundation, of which I am a trustee, put up $40,000 for a deposit on the van. Normally we give just small cash grants of $500 to $1,000 to people in emergencies, but this case seemed to merit more. Chris had done so much in her life to help herself—but this time she needed help from others.

That was Labor Day, and by Christmas we had raised the rest of the money—all by e-mail, without using a single postage stamp! Here's how we did it: We sent out fifty e-mails to people we knew, people who trusted us. We explained the situation and told them, "We promise you that every cent you send us will go to pay for the van. Not a penny will go to administration, not even postage!" We also asked them to go one step further: "Send this e-mail to ten people you know who trust you. Make the same promise to them that we made to you, and request that they pass along the request to ten more people who trust them." This was important—we were building a *community of trust*. There are so many fund-raising scams out there, we needed for people to trust us and to trust one another.

We kept our promise, and they kept theirs. For the first two weeks, we received checks from people we knew. But by the third week, we were starting to get money from people whose names we didn't recognize. The network was working, and our community of trust was doing its job.

What made this feat all the more remarkable was that it happened at a time when the San Diego area was ravaged by the worst wildfires in our history. It was a terrible time to try to raise money. People were feeling helpless and hopeless in the face of such a community disaster. This is a common problem—people get so overwhelmed in the face of others' need that they often do nothing. They think, "What can I do? I'm just one person." It's the same reason many people don't vote. They don't think that one person can make a difference or that what they have to offer counts.

Our story is bigger than just getting a new Freedom Van for Chris—it's the story of showing people that they *can* make a difference, even if it's just sending in $1, or $5, or $10. We got a lot of small contributions in those months. We don't need a big, important, wealthy donor—we just needed lots of individuals, regular folks, to give what they could. Our project has the same message as Chris's entire life: We are not paralyzed as people—there is always something we can do, no matter how big the problem. By taking action, any action, people can overcome their own personal sense of paralysis.

We didn't need one person to give us $70,000—we would have been happier to get 70,000 people to give just $1 each. People are glad to be part of something that makes a difference. If everyone did this kind of thing all the time—asked themselves, What little thing can I do to contribute to others?—and if everybody picked just one other person to help, the world would be transformed.

For us, the next project we want to take on is transforming that dumb law that says each disabled person can only have one state-sponsored van in their lifetime. Anyone want to join us in making a difference with that?

For further information, contact Cathy Conheim at *www.realwomen.org.*

—Cathy Conheim

My friends have made the story of my life. In a thousand ways, they've turned my limitations into beautiful privileges.

—Helen Keller, inspirational writer who was deaf and blind

That which is shareable, is bearable.

—Jeanne Segal, therapist, author

COMMUNITY: *What's in a Word?*

Coming together

Open arms, open hearts, open minds

Mutual respect

Mutual support

Understanding differences

Never losing sight of common goals

Integrity—both individual and collective

Trust and truth

Yearning for healthy interdependence

Carrying the Message

THE IDEA CAME TO ME one day over lunch with a male friend. It was 1983, before Gorbachev had come to power in the USSR. My friend and I were talking about world events and seemingly intractable problems in various countries around the world. I had seen firsthand the ravages of alcohol in families and communities in the United States. In Russia, it seemed, an entire country was in the grips of alcoholism. I had also seen the miracles that take place through the twelve steps of recovery in Alcoholics Anonymous— in my own life, and in the lives of many others. "Wouldn't it be wonderful if they had AA in the Soviet Union?" I asked my lunch partner. He looked stunned, stood up, and said, "Faith, that's a terrific idea! Do it, Faith, do it!"

It scared me. Where did this idea come from? It seemed like way too much for just one person to undertake. After all, I was over sixty at this point. So I did nothing. I just sat on the idea . . . for two years. It nagged me. It wouldn't go away.

A couple years later I was taking a weekend communication seminar with about 200 other people, including several of my six adult children. At the end of the seminar, each person stood and made a commitment, based on what they'd learned in their time together. When my turn came, I opened my mouth and out came, "I want to do this—and I don't want to do this. I'm taking a stand to establish AA in the Soviet Union, and to get it off the ground in two months." As I sat down, I noticed I was shaking.

A woman came up to me after the seminar adjourned and she said, "Faith, I'm an attorney and I'm going to align with your stand." That immediate affirmation gave me the reinforcement I needed. It also helped that I had made this commitment in front of all those other people, including my kids. Their support was to encourage me in the months and years to come.

From then on, I knew that I would do it. I encountered criticism in the AA community. Some said that I was violating AA's tradition of growing by "attraction rather than promotion." Others accused me of "going there to help the enemy." I listened politely to everyone's concerns, but I just knew I had to do it.

I had fliers made and handed them out at AA meetings. I invited people to my home to talk about the idea and how we might make it a reality. I was looking for support. How were we going to do this? We had no role models to follow, we knew we would have to make it up as we went along. We gave our project a name, "Creating a Sober World" (CASW).

We used inspirational quotes from famous people to keep ourselves going. People like the American dancer, Martha Graham. She said when some idea or vision comes through you, you're responsible for making it happen. If not, it'll be lost forever. I agree with that. I always say that the idea would not come through you if you didn't have the ability to manifest it. So many people have great ideas and lofty visions, but they do nothing and the potential is lost—we give up on ourselves.

My AA friends and I created a pledge for ourselves: An opportunity to participate in creating a possibility within an impossibility.

Then we set a vision: To create the first AA open speaker meeting in Moscow with government approval.

We made a commitment: To be willing to work on the committee that would see the vision manifest by June 6, 1986.

At first we met and just floundered. We had no idea what we were doing. Then we started to get our act together. We sent letters to "movers and shakers" of the world; we reassured them we weren't asking for money—we were asking for support, advice, suggestions, and opportunities to make connections with the right people who could help us.

Our group changed a bit, as some people dropped out and new people took their places. We finally stabilized at about twenty members. One of our members knew of two women in San Francisco, Sharon Tennison and Sarah Seybold, who had taken lots of groups to the USSR. I went to visit them at their Center for US-USSR Initiatives. They caught fire with our project and offered to lead us on our first trip.

In November 1985, we made our first trip to Moscow, where we met with Dr. Andrei Petukhov from the USSR Ministry of Health. We had prepared for our trip by learning as much as we could about Russian customs, history, and culture. We learned a few phrases in Russian. Sharon and Sarah had taken some of our AA literature to Dr. Petukhov in a previous trip, and based on early feedback, we were concerned that the use of "God," "Higher Power," and "spiritual awakening" might be a stumbling block to establishing AA in the officially atheistic Soviet society.

But Dr. Petukhov surprised us. After hearing my own story of recovery, and having read our literature, he turned to me and said, "Mrs. _____, our government has no problem whatsoever with you bringing Alcoholics Anonymous into our country." I cried tears of joy.

We came back to the United States and got busy preparing for the next stage of our project—to take a team of people back with us and start holding AA meetings in Moscow. The Soviets had requested that we change our start date to April 5, 1986, so we had to accelerate our work to be ready in time. It was exhilarating *and* exhausting!

Thirty of us made that historic trip—ranging in age from eighteen to seventy-two. We came from all over the country—California, Connecticut, Hawaii, Idaho, New York, Missouri, Texas. We wore big yellow buttons that we had made, with the AA logo and "One Day at a Time" in Russian. These buttons served as terrific icebreakers with Soviet physicians, government leaders, journalists, citizens, and all those whose support we needed to make AA successful in their country. We held several AA meetings that first month, in different cities with different groups in attendance. Not only did we need to carry the message to the alcoholics, we needed to educate their whole society about the possibility of an answer to the scourge of Soviet alcoholism.

One doctor, who had been reluctant to come to one of our meetings, said he had never seen his patients share in the clinic as they did following the Americans' example. His final words were, "We have a common problem, there is a common solution, and we must work together."

There were so many individual experiences, miraculous in their happenings—that I could go on and on. But suffice it to say that it was clear we would need to make many return visits to the USSR to help support our fledgling friends in recovery. For several years, we went back on a quarterly basis. As the years went by, less often.

Today, the Soviet Union is no more. The end of communism and the breakup of the former members of the USSR has changed the face of that part of the world forever. But while communism is dead, AA is still very much alive, with hundreds of meetings and tens of thousands of people who are now leading sober lives.

A vision that began with one person, who was scared to death by the possibility she had uttered, became a reality because of the commitment of a community of kindred spirits. My AA friends are people who have devoted their lives to carrying the message to the alcoholic who still suffers, wherever he or she may be. The Iron Curtain was not impenetrable to a community of such committed souls.

—Faith.

Compassion is the basis for all morality.
—Arthur Schopenhauer, Polish-born philosopher

The Goddess Gang

IN THE MID-'80s, my friend Mo and I had the good fortune to be invited to a weekend with Joan Halifax entitled "Reemergence of the Goddess." Three to four hundred women participated and it was the most amazing experience. (Of course, goddess talk today is commonplace, but back then it was totally new.) There were women like Deena Metzger, Marija Gimbutas, among others—women who had been to the mountain and come back with sacred information to share with the rest of us.

It was a life-changing event for me. It was the first time in my life I had been friendly in a public setting like that. It was my first experience of goddess energy, of being in the presence of powerful feminine energy. It was my first experience of "sacred time." I had a notebook with me and I began collecting names, addresses, and phone numbers, because I wanted to keep in touch with these phenomenal women. Somehow I knew that this was a watershed event, and I wanted to find a way to keep it going in my life.

When we got home, Mo and I decided to contact all these women and see who might be interested in forming a Goddess Gang that would meet on an ongoing basis to continue the sacred work we had begun that weekend. A number of women responded. Mo had a friend who had a big house, and we started meeting there regularly. At first we got heavily involved in Native American spirituality, because Jolene, one of our members, had studied with Harley Swift Deer. Others had studied with Carlos Castañeda, and some were working with a variety of other Native American heal-ers and shamans. This was meaningful work for me, because I had been alienated from my Presbyterian upbringing, and discovered a new faith—a faith in nature. I realized that God isn't in a book—God is in the trees from which the book is made. I became able to see the true power of the universe in the natural world, and it was thrilling.

Over time, the group distilled itself down to thirteen women. Deborah, who had a big, beautiful home in Nichols Canyon, sug-gested we move our meetings there, so we did.

And after that, we really started to *work*. I hated it, but I couldn't not do it. I had a very busy life, as did all thirteen of the women, and I often resented having to drive the distance to Deborah's home, of having to prepare some food, or to bring some sacred objects for a ceremony—but then I would get to the gathering and it was always wonderful, and powerful. I discovered that learning and growing always involves stretching and doing that which is *not* convenient and easy.

We invited various teachers to come work with us—Lynn Andrews, Joan Halifax, teachers of various traditions, including some wonderful Buddhist teachers. We would sit in a circle in our beautiful clothes—we all dressed up for our meetings, usually in some flowing kind of gowns or dresses. We ate exquisite food that we had each prepared. It was never planned, as in "three people bring salads, two bring dessert"—the right food just showed up, and it was always incredible. There was no alcohol or drugs. We weren't about getting high, it was about "getting down."

Sure, there were tensions, dramas, and even a little gossip—women being women, after all. There were the life challenges that various members were going through at various times. We discovered that our own mothers had all been bereft and broken in some way, and the Goddess Gang was able to give each of us what our mothers never could.

One of the most powerful exercises we did was a Star Maiden Circle, which seemed to happen around the time of someone's birthday. A woman would sit in the center of the circle, facing one woman at a time. She would ask, "What do I want to give up? What do I aspire to? What am I afraid of? What do I want?" This is very effective, for the only way you can discover yourself is in the reflection of someone else's eyes. We would hold the space for each person, so that she could answer her own questions and discover who she really was.

I recall one night when we were all sitting in a circle by candlelight. I looked around and noticed that everyone was so *beautiful*—in their flowing gowns, their hair just so, their faces glowing in the soft light. Then I realized—if they're so beautiful, then I must be too! That's the door I went through, and once you do, you can't go back. You've seen your own beauty and you're never the same. Things change as a result.

This whole experience was divinely ordained, I am convinced. It was and is a holy thing. We don't meet as often as we used to—now it's maybe once a year or so. We all went out into the world, our baggage considerably lighter, and our self-love and self-assurance markedly stronger. We're still in touch, and I know we'll get together soon. Thank Goddess for the transformative spiritual power of women in community!

—Lindsay Smith

Women best understand each other's language.
—Teresa of Avila, Spanish Carmelite nun, mystic, saint

It is not meaningless that we enjoy games which demand a high degree of teamwork.
—Pearl S. Buck, author

Finding the Tribe

The yurt opened into the swift air of autumn. I crouched to exit, grabbed my lunch, and settled beneath a tree to eat. Other women, herbal apprentices whose life stories had warmed the morning circle, joined me. The conversation rounded the topic of friendship.

"I don't really have any women friends," one young mother surprised me by saying. "Although I would like a woman friend, the only woman I get along with is my sister. Even though we fight all the time, I love her."

"Perhaps," I offered, "you could expand your definition of sister."

—Joey Garcia

Friendship—any close friendship—is so various, made up of so many strands; companionship, the sharing of laughter, common work, and common tastes.
　　—Iris Origo, Anglo-American biographer, historian

Never forget that when we are silent, we are one. When we speak, we are two.
　—Indira Gandhi, Prime Minister of India

The meeting of two personalities is like the contact of two chemical substances: if there is any reaction, both are transformed.
　　—Carl Jung, Swiss psychologist

RAINBOW SOCKS PROJECT

"THOSE WOMEN AND CHILDREN are freezing. What can I do?" Babbi Cameron asked herself in the mid-1990s. The war was raging in Bosnia, winter was upon them, and Babbi wanted to help. "What can one woman in Boston do to help people halfway 'round the world?" she wondered. She knew firsthand the biting cold of snowy winters, since Boston isn't exactly in the temperate climate zone. She knew that fingers and toes were especially vulnerable to frigid temperatures and frostbite. She decided that mittens and socks would be a big help to the folks struggling through a winter made worse by war.

Babbi Cameron was just one woman, but she quickly attracted others who wanted to help. Her idea was to send yarn and knitting needles to the women of Bosnia, so that they could knit socks and mittens for their families and friends. I heard about Babbi from my sister-in-law Julie, who sent me a letter one day about what had become known as the Rainbow Socks Project. "Would you be interested in helping these women?" Julie asked me. She knew me well.

As the months went by, it was discovered that the village had made enough mittens, socks, booties, and other knitwear to get them through the winter. But there were so many other needs still unmet. Babbi decided the solution was to start buying back the socks and mittens from the Bosnian women, so they would have cash for food, supplies, and rebuilding their bombed-out village. I thought this was a great idea, and decided that I would buy the knitwear from Babbi and sell it in my catalog, "Femail Creations." Babbi would send them yarn and knitting needles, then buy back the knitwear they produced, and I, in turn, would buy the goods from Babbi and resell them to my customers.

Giving back has always been at the heart of Femail Creations. With each of the five catalogs we publish each year, we adopt a worthwhile charity to promote. I just loved the idea of the Rainbow Socks Project. I chose to feature the Rainbow Socks Project as our "Making a Difference" charity for the holiday issue of Femail Creations. Our customers loved the socks! Each one unique, knitted with patterns handed down through the generations. Our customers told their friends, and the word spread like wildfire. The mittens and socks were best-sellers. That's what happens when women come together around a cause.

We sold tens of thousands of dollars worth of colorful, warm, charming hand-knitted woolens—and were able to send that money over to Bosnia to help these women. It was amazing how much our check was able to buy in Bosnia. Babbi used her personal frequent flyer miles to fly over to Bosnia to give them the money in person.

When she returned, she brought me a handwritten thank-you note from the village, along with a piece of beautiful fabric. She translated the letter for me. "They have a special name for you over there," she told me. "They call you 'the good woman.'" Tears welled up in my eyes as she read me their letter.

"And this fabric—I want to tell you about this fabric," she continued. "They were able to use some of the money you raised from your catalog sales to buy a loom. And with that loom, they are able to weave fine fabric, which they can sell and make more money for their village. They wanted you to have the very first piece of fabric off their new loom."

I love to tell this story because it's like that piece of fabric—it starts with a single thread, and when woven together with other threads, grows and becomes big enough to cover a whole village. It starts with one woman in Boston who asked herself, "People are freezing in Bosnia. What can I do?" She enlisted the help of all her friends, who then got their friends involved. Then my dear sister-in-law got me involved, and I got all my catalog customers involved. It wove itself, from a simple thread into a beautiful tapestry. It's about the power of individuals, working together/woven together, into a tapestry that wraps 'round the world.

—Lisa Hammond

I believe in the dependence of people upon each other. I believe in the light and warmth of human affection, the disinterested acts of kindness, and the compassion of complete strangers.

—Iris Origo, Anglo-American biographer, historian

And Finally . . .
In my experience, true friends:

ACCEPT you, warts and all

BELIEVE in your potential

COMFORT you when you're sad

DELIGHT in your successes

EMPATHIZE with your struggles

FORGIVE you when you hurt their feelings, just as
you do for them

GIVE you time and attention

HUG you . . . often

INSPIRE you to do your best

JUST LOVE YOU

KEEP your secrets

LISTEN with their hearts

MAKE you want to be a better person

NEVER judge you

OCCASIONALLY disappoint you, 'cause they're
human, too

POINT out your good qualities when you forget

QUESTION you when you're about to do something
   really dumb

RESPECT your boundaries

SHARE their hopes and fears with you

TELL you the truth

UNDERSTAND you, even when you don't understand
   yourself

VALUE your ideas and opinions

WILL DO anything they can to help you

XTEND you the benefit of the doubt

YEARN to hear from you when you're away

ZING with joy 'cause you're their friend

Thank You

Dear friends,

Books come into being in different ways . . . usually the author has an idea and goes in search of a publisher. But in this case, my creative publisher, Jan Johnson, and Conari's marketing maven, Brenda Knight, badgered me into writing this book. "We just love your first book . . . you have to write another one for us," they cajoled. I resisted. They persisted. I ignored. They implored. Finally . . . they won. And I'm glad they did. Thank you, Jan, for your editorial guidance, your imagination, and your ability to see that there was another book in me that I didn't know was there. And thank you, beautiful bountiful Brenda, for your enthusiasm, encouragement, and persistence. How can anyone ever resist you?

I want to extend an enormous "Thank you" to the wise, witty, wonderful women who have shared their friendship stories with me. Their names are in their stories, so I won't list them all here. Just know that in this book and in my life, friends really are everything.

"Thank you" to all the fabulous women at Conari—Kate Hartke, Bonni Hamilton, Emily Logan, Bethany Michalski, Jill Rogers, Kathleen Fivel, Liz Wood, and Rachel Leach (oh yes, you too, Michael Kerber and Mike Conlon!). And a big hug of thanks to my terrific publicist, Leslie Rossman. It takes a Bevy of Babes to make a book successful!

My deepest thanks to my two best friends on the planet—my mother Gloria and my son Michael. I may be a writer, and I may be good with words, but words fail me when I try to say how much I love you.

And finally, a loving "Thank you" to all the friends in my life—you know who you are.

Thank you one and all!

With love and laughter,

BJ

About the Author

BJ Gallagher is a storyteller, both by inclination and by profession. Her Irish heritage blessed her with a natural gift of gab, and her stories enrich and enliven the presentations she makes to groups of all sizes. "People forget facts and figures," she says, "but they remember good stories." BJ uses stories to teach important lessons about how to live a good life, create authentic friendships, nurture happy families, and do fulfilling work in the world.

Her own life story is as eclectic as the collection in this book. The daughter of a military family, she was "drafted at birth." She has lived in four countries on three continents, and in six states within the United States, from one of the littlest (Delaware) to one of the biggest (Texas). Although a native Californian, she is at home anywhere in the world. Her working life has run the gamut from cocktail waitress to corporate middle manager, including stints as intern in a congressman's office, secretary for a studio of graphic artists, sales trainer for car dealerships, ghost writer for a corporate CEO, career counselor, and university adjunct professor. She has been a stay-at-home wife as well as a single working mother with a latch-key kid. She is a Phi Beta Kappa graduate of the University of Southern California, and earned her advanced degree from the School of Hard Knocks. Her crazy-quilt life has provided her with ample opportunity to hear and learn from other people's stories.

BJ has written ten books, including the international best-seller, *A Peacock in the Land of Penguins* (now published in 17 languages worldwide; 400,000 copies sold). She gives keynote speeches for women's groups as well as corporate clients and professional associations. Her company, Peacock Productions, provides training programs, as well as books, videos, and other training materials and services to human resource professionals. Her other recent books are *Everything I Need to Know I Learned from Other Women* and *Who Are "They" Anyway?*

For more information, contact BJ in Los Angeles at (323) 227-6205 or visit her websites: *www.womenneed2know.com* and *www.peacockproductions.com*.

To Our Readers

CONARI PRESS, an imprint of Red Wheel/Weiser, publishes books on topics ranging from spirituality, personal growth, and relationships to women's issues, parenting, and social issues. Our mission is to publish quality books that will make a difference in people's lives—how we feel about ourselves and how we relate to one another. We value integrity, compassion, and receptivity, both in the books we publish and in the way we do business.

Our readers are our most important resource, and we value your input, suggestions, and ideas about what you would like to see published. Please feel free to contact us, to request our latest book catalog, or to be added to our mailing list.

Conari Press
An imprint of Red Wheel/Weiser, LLC
P.O. Box 612
York Beach, ME 03910-0612
www.conari.com